D0442954

101
CHAMPAGNES

101

CHAMPAGNES

and other sparkling wines

TO TRY BEFORE YOU DIE

DAVY ŻYW

BIRLINN

First published in Great Britain in 2018 by
Birlinn Ltd

West Newington House
10 Newington Road
Edinburgh
EH9 1QS

www.birlinn.co.uk

ISBN: 978 1 78027 556 7

British Library Cataloguing-in-Publication Data
A catalogue record for this book is available on request from the British Library

Designed and typeset by Teresa Monachino

Printed and Bound in Latvia by PnB

★ Contents

ORDRE DES COTEAUX DE
CHAMPAGNE
Ambassade du Royaume-Uni
www.ordredescoteaux.com

Preface: Fizz and Me

★

I HAVE WORKED WITHIN WINE FOR OVER A DECADE. I STARTED IN A basement wine shop in Edinburgh, then became a *sommelier* in famous restaurants. More recently I have been wine development manager for the world's second largest wine retailer, a global wine buyer for a leading wine retailer and now a wine buyer at the world's most famous vintner. In 2018, I was sworn into the ancient Ordre des Coteaux du Champagne as a Chevalier, so I know what I'm talking about! I live out of a suitcase, blending, tasting and travelling wherever the grapes and vintages take me. My friends hate me. However, working in restaurants is where my real love of flavour and wine was nurtured. I loved the showmanship, pace and energy of being a *somm*. It was in fine-dining restaurants where I was lucky enough to taste some of the most exquisite and expensive wines and champagnes. Wine can raise a plate from a forgettable dinner into a memorable, taste-bud-tantalising experience. What I love about champagne is the dynamic it brings to a meal. The fizz alters textures, cuts through or combines fats and proteins and lifts flavours to another level. Champagne with food is one of life's true delights.

Flavour can change perceptions, incite memories, alter moods, bring people together and divide the best of friends. Sourcing and blending wine for a living, I have made a career in combining flavours and textures to enhance pleasure, enjoyment and gastronomic experience. I cannot taste for you but I can recommend what I think you will enjoy. In the following pages I'll offer suggestions as to what you might like to eat both to enhance the pleasure of the wine you are drinking and to improve the taste of what you are eating.

Lots of people would enjoy wine more if it were demystified a little. Wine is made to be enjoyed by everyone, and even the smallest amount of knowledge will empower imbibers to make the right choices. This book will add to your drinking and dining experience – and doubles up as a terrific coaster.

Introduction

★

CHAMPAGNE IS DELICIOUS. THIS IS VERY IMPORTANT. IT'S SCRUMPTIOUS and magnificent. We love its flavour; we love its fizziness. We love the sense of drama and celebration it brings to any occasion. Champagne's associations with success, partying and enjoyment are as ingrained in the wine as the bubbles themselves. As the godfather of champagne famously said: 'Brothers, I'm drinking stars!' Dom Pérignon had obviously had a few glasses at this point, but his quote is poignant nonetheless: drinking champagne is liquid heaven.

I want to share with you my passion for the fizz, and in doing so give insight into how champagne has earned its eternally glamorous status, and why sparkling wine and champagne are the drinks with which we celebrate life. It marks our milestones, in a way no other drink can. There is always an excited intake of breath when the bottle pops. Most champagne bottles have close to 6 atmospheric bars of pressure within them, a similar pressure found in a double-decker bus tyre. This danger and tension in opening a bottle is unique to champagne; it is both sexy and dramatic. It gets the party started.

But for all the drama and allure, ultimately it's the drink itself which has made champagne such an irresistible choice for millions of drinkers over the past four centuries. It hasn't been one long party for the people of the Champagne region of north-east France, however. Wines have been made there since Roman times but their look and taste have changed over those millennia. The region, and its wines, have had a turbulent history: revolutions, a couple of invasions, economic turmoil, two world wars and a devastating vineyard pest. Times have been tough, and, like the production of champagne itself, this has been no quick process; it has taken time, sweat, blood, tears and a helluvalotta love. This history makes it all the more marvellous that champagne has survived and thrived.

For all its success, champagne is a misunderstood drink. Its purely celebratory positioning has meant we tend to focus on the luxurious larger brands, instead of exploring the range for our more frequent drinking habits. Many of the most famous champagne houses have a place at my table but the world of sparkling wine is evolving rapidly, even within the Champagne region. More and more small growers are producing quality champagnes, and the diversity and quality from the region is exciting.

But champagne is not the only magnificent sparkling wine available – we have never had so much choice in finding our favourite fizzer. Many champagne makers have taken their trade all around the world, finding new methods, grapes and climates to producer fine examples from Australia, California and South America. There are many other sparkling wines which offer parallel quality and terrific value, from the rural slopes of the Jura, to where it all started in the land-locked hills of the Languedoc, and even to the lava dashed slopes of Mount Etna. Catalunya is home to cava, where the styles and quality have never been so good. And, back in the UK, the English sparkling wine business is booming. Many wines are now beating champagnes in blind tastings and awards, and I celebrate some of them in this book.

The UK is historically one of the largest markets for champagne and sparkling wine in the world. We love bubbles. And, although we have begun to make our own we are still the sixth largest importer of sparkling wine in the world today. The incredible success story of prosecco has opened doors for many of us to drink and try new sparkling wines, without breaking the bank. In the UK prosecco has become a go-to drink, and many prefer it to champagne.

There are so many amazing sparkling wines in the world, and my 101 recommendations are a great place to start. Get those glasses poised.

★ **DID YOU KNOW?**
There are 49 million bubbles in every bottle of champagne.

Origins and early doors

★

HISTORY CREDITS THE SEVENTEENTH-CENTURY DOM PIERRE PÉRIGNON with discovering the magic and secret of champagne's bubbles at the Benedictine Abbey of Hautvillers. The story goes that in the dark, damp chalky cellars, the monk managed to metamorphose the local still wine into the sparkling liquid gold wine we know today. However endearing this might be, it couldn't be farther from the truth. Dom Pérignon was certainly an exceptional wine taster, winemaker and grape grower, but his job at Hautvillers Abbey was not to create a new wine but to get rid of the naturally occurring bubbles which were ruining the quality still wines that formed his fellow monks' profitable business. If he had been successful in his job, champagne might have never existed. Champagne, the first commercial sparkling wine, wasn't an overnight discovery, but developed and evolved over centuries, driven by human endeavour.

If you think sparkling wine was invented in Champagne you would be wrong about that too. Like many of the best ideas, the invention of fizzy wine was a total accident. For the birth of sparkling wines we must turn to a little unknown town in the south of France.

Limoux is a small, mountain-locked town in the Languedoc-Roussillon area of Mediterranean France. The first written record of Limoux's sparkling wine Blanquette de Limoux is in 1531 at the abbey of Saint-Hilaire, but it is likely that the wines had been made for some time previously. At this point champagne didn't exist, and this was over a century before the birth of Dom Pérignon. Like a lot of wines and spirits in Europe at the time, the wines of Limoux were made by Benedictine monks. Many of the spectacular monasteries you see across the continent were directly funded by booze.

Until the late 1700s the sparkling wines of Limoux and Champagne were made in a similar way to today's artisan cider. After pressing the grapes, natural yeasts found in the winery would begin fermenting the grape juice into wine, converting the sugars of the grapes into alcohol. For fermentation you need a steady, pleasant temperature; otherwise the yeasts give up and go dormant, which would have happened over the cold winters of 1500s rural France. This meant the wines were bottled even though the fermentation process was hibernating during the cold winter months. Then spring came and kickstarted the process again. There are two main by-products of a wine's fermentation: alcohol and CO_2 gas. So, when the weather warmed up and the yeasts got back to work, the fermentation would carry on, converting the remaining sugars into alcohol and trapping the CO_2 in the bottle, dissolving it into the wine . . . and *voilà*: sparkling wine.

At the beginning, this process was haphazard and totally accidental. Back then the glass used for bottles was not as strong as it is today, so when a thirsty monk went down into the cellar in the spring, he would find a lot of his precious wine bottles had exploded and smashed. For a long time champagne was called Devil's Wine, because of the danger associated with the exploding bottles, which were responsible for many deaths. It would take hundreds of years to streamline and develop this process (now called *méthode traditionnelle*) in the chalk cellars of Champagne, making it safe and reliable. Outside of the Champagne region, modern technology has allowed winemakers to make sparkling wines by other means, creating wines which are more efficient to produce, less labour intensive and cheaper to make. These wines are made in one tank, rather than in individual bottles. The most famous of these wines is prosecco.

★ **DID YOU KNOW?**
It is maintained that the reason wine bottles are 75cl is because this was the average breath of a glass blower.

The breakthrough moment for all champagne production came in the nineteenth century, when a local French pharmacist, André François, trialled and discovered the precise measurement of sugar needed to create the sparkle in the bottles, without producing too much pressure. This is when champagne became the success story it is today. Production boomed from a mere 300,000 bottles a year to 20 million by the mid nineteenth century. Today close to 340 million bottles are produced each year.

Champagne's real success is a post-war phenomenon. In the late nineteenth and early twentieth centuries, the Champagne region had to contend with severe setbacks. Phylloxera, a vine louse, ate 99% of all the vines in the region, which meant the entire area had to be replanted by grafting on resistant roots. This devastated the world of wine, and its effect can still be felt in the champagne and wine industry today. Some champagne houses (such as Louis Roederer and Moët & Chandon) had the foresight to purchase prime-situated vines when the prices were rock bottom. Nowadays, the real estate in Champagne is some of the most expensive in the world: for a block of vines in the Côte des Blancs you would pay the same price as for a penthouse in Manhattan.

After the First World War, two of the largest markets collapsed due to the revolution in Russia and Prohibition, which stopped most sales into America from 1920 until 1933. The enterprising Champenois had to look elsewhere to sell their wines, and successfully achieved this in Germany and Britain, which are still the most important export markets for Champagne. The United Kingdom is the most important market outside France.

★ **DID YOU KNOW?**
Up until a couple of years ago London drank more champagne than the entire United States.

Spicy Red

Bold Red/
Bordeaux Glass

Aromatic Red/
Burgundy Glass

Light White

Bold White

One Size Fits All

Tulip (sparkling

Flute (sparkling)

Coupe
(sparkling/cocktails)

Sweet Fortified

Sweet White

Dry Fortified

> *Any of these glass shapes can be used for drinking champers.*
> *I'd recommend the tulip or light white glass for everyday use,*
> *and a bold white glass for older champagnes.*

Know your glasses

★

If you really want to get maximum enjoyment out of your champagne or sparkling wine, it helps to have proper glassware.

The shapes and sizes of glasses have shifted, following changes in drinking status, trends and fashions, and with an improved understanding of the flavour of champagne. Generally speaking champagne glasses are designed to enhance and accentuate a particular organoleptic quality found in the wine, while keeping your hot hands away from the liquid to avoid warming your delicately cooled champagne. This is why wine glasses have long stems.

There are three main factors influencing the shape of glass:

1. *Air.* The ratio of oxygen to wine is important – the more surface of the wine that is exposed, the more aromas and smells that are released. A fine balance is needed, as too much oxygen can let all the bubbles escape too quickly and allows the aromas to disappear too easily.
2. *Shape.* The shape of the glass will channel aromas and smells in the right direction, i.e. up your schnoz. The shape will also dictate the persistence and display of bubbles: the narrower and taller the glass, the smaller the ratio of air to wine, keeping those cheeky bubbles alive for longer.
3. *Style.* Champagne is a symbol of status. If you drive a Rolls Royce, you park it where people can see it. Many people who drink champagne want everyone to know they are drinking champagne. The best way to do this is to waft and wave your coupes or flutes around the place.

Ciao ciao coupe!

The most famous of champagne's glasses has to be the shallow coupe, said to be modelled on the breasts of France's queen Marie Antoinette. Although this glass was actually created specifically for sparkling wine in England in the 1690s, I still like to think Marie Antoinette's desirable bosom had a part to play in the design. The coupe became hugely popular in the UK, the States and Russia, glamorised by champagne houses, including Veuve Clicquot. The problem with the coupe glass is that it is too short and too wide. Once poured, the champagne goes flat a little too quickly.

Farewell to flutes!

Flutes are popular because they showcase the tiny, gently rising bubbles up the sides of a tall, narrow glass, thus continuing champagne's visual appeal. The best flutes have etching in the bottom of the glass to act as a nucleation point for the steady, even stream of bubbles. Another major plus for the flute is that it's much harder to spill your precious fizz out of the glass.

But although flutes are visually pleasing, they do not best showcase the quality of champagne in the glass; in fact they impede it. They are fine for simple fizzers at parties, but if you have a special bottle you want to savour, then flutes will literally restrict the flavour. Like fine wine, a certain amount of oxygen is needed to open and aerate the aromas and flavours. The shape of the flute inhibits the style, and can hide the taste. I'm happier drinking my champers out of normal wine glasses so that I can fully appreciate the aromas and tastes released in the glass. I recommend you follow suit.

'drinking from flutes is like listening to a concert in ear muffs'.
MAGGIE HENRIQUES, CEO OF KRUG

Time for the tulip

With the shift away from flutes and coupes, many of the top champagne houses have devised bespoke glasses for their own top cuvées. When I visited Dom Pérignon, we tasted (drank) out of bulb-shaped glasses with a tapered lip, more similar to burgundy glasses. The perfect glass for champagne was devised between head sommelier in Reims' top Michelin restaurant, Les Crayères, and the town's university. The result is a tulip-shaped glass which offers the best of both flutes and wine glasses. Basically, the glass is made to respect the role of the mousse or effervescence found in the champagne, which carries more of the flavour aromas than the liquid itself. The shape of the tulip glass gives more air to the surface of the champagne, thus allowing more of the fizzy aromas to escape, then cleverly tapers around the rim to allow each one of the bubbles to burst simultaneously at the glass's widest point. So, when you stick your nose in for a whiff, you get maximum flavour and aromas from the bursting champagne bubbles. BOOM!

Many sparkling wines, especially champagnes, have taken years or decades to make. It would be a shame to undo all that time in a few seconds by using the wrong vessel. So, next time you pop a cork, do yourself a flavour favour and use a proper glass.

Fizz with food

★

Food and wine matching isn't taken very seriously in the UK, an afterthought at best, but if you follow a few simple principles it can lift an ordinary meal and glass of wine into a gastronomic extravaganza. There are countless books on the principles of food and wine matching; you could write a bloody dissertation on it – I did! But as any *sommelier* will tell you, you can't learn anything without trial and error: eating, drinking and evaluating.

At the most basic level, food and wine matching serves one purpose: to enhance enjoyment of what you are eating and drinking. It does this by combining or contrasting the tastes and flavours of a dish to the wine, utilising taste attributes of a dish (sweetness, bitterness, acidity, astringency, saltiness and fattiness) to bring out desired flavours in both food and wine. This works for two reasons:

1. *Balance.* A good food and wine match should be balanced, which means you can taste everything from the dish and wine harmoniously, making it even more delicious.
2. *Gusto.* A good food and wine match should create more flavour and more taste for the diner, i.e. you get more out of each component on the plate or in the glass than you would when you taste them separately. This means a food and wine match will taste better than the sum of its parts: 1 + 1 = 3 so to speak.

The fundamental difficulty with food and wine matching is the unknown of what the wine will taste like, and the risk of parting with money for a stab in the dark – I've been burnt before! If you are buying a bottle from the supermarket shelf or wine shop, unless you know the wine it is almost impossible to know exactly how it's going to taste, even if you do read the back label. In good wine retailers, there is help on hand – use it. In fancy restaurants this is the role of a *sommelier* or *somm*:

to match the desired flavour of a wine to the customer's wants (and budget), to enhance the plate of food that the chef has cooked.

Champagne and sparkling wine are usually opened as an aperitif before dinner, for two reasons. First, it gets you buzzed quicker, as the alcohol bursting in the bubbles enters your bloodstream faster than through your stomach lining. And, secondly, champagne stimulates taste buds: the acidity and bitterness of champagne make you salivate, so it actually makes you thirstier and hungrier. After we finish our flute, and eat one too many canapés, we tend to move on to other wines. But why stop the party there? Champagne and good sparkling wine with the correct food is bliss. It shouldn't be forgotten that champagne has all the same elements as the still variety. Sparkling wine brings a fresh dynamic to any meal because the fizz brings texture in the form of mousse, often carrying a level of astringency and bitterness which, paired with rich, fatty or salty flavours, makes for a delicious combination. Acidity is one of champagne's key pillars, hugely desirable for food and wine matches, as it brings freshness. If you are eating fatty or salty foods, you need acidity to balance the heaviness and richness of texture and flavour from the fat. We use acidity like this every day, for example malt vinegar on your chips or lemon juice on your fish.

Champagne and other sparklers also bring sweetness. This level of sweetness, paired with the acidity, means champagne is an incredibly versatile food companion. If your dish is salty, a touch of sweetness in your wine can work wonderfully well. For example; a fatty, salty cheeseburger benefits from sweet and acidic tomato ketchup; dry sparkling wine brings the same principle to any dish.

Champagne and other *méthode traditionnelle* sparkling wine like English Sparkling or cava have a unique flavour: toastiness. This delicious flavour spectrum brings a different element to any plate of food, and like bread it is a versatile flavour. Whether you are eating soup, starter, main course or dessert, champagne can be drunk with them all.

Two things to keep in mind when choosing a champagne to pair with your meal: age and style. Generally, the older a champagne, the richer and fuller it is going to be, so it can be paired with more wholesome, savoury and richer dishes. Younger styles are fresher tasting, and tend to work with lighter, crunchier dishes. For instance, the younger English sparkling wines are fantastic with oysters, chips or creamy caesar salad because of their fresh flavour and high acidity; older vintage champagne could complete a roast chicken (richer dish).

A simpler sparkling wine, such as prosecco, is often just drunk on its own without the need for food, but can also be a delightful pairing with a host of lighter dishes: salty olives, canapés, summer salads, grilled chicken or even fruity desserts, because of the bright acidity and sweetness.

Rosé champagnes carry all the traits of normal champagne, and more. Depending on the production methods, rosés tend to have bolder red fruit characters to match with richer dishes, sweet or savoury. Many rosés are made with a proportion of still red wine, so the flavours found in them can be more akin to Burgundian red wine, and tend to have fuller, savoury character. This means you can enjoy them on their own, but they are also hugely versatile food companions. You can throw a lot of flavour-rich foods at rosés, meaty or fruity, and be rewarded: Thai crab cakes, steak tartare, pink rack of lamb, beetroot salsa and even fruity desserts.

Sparkling reds are another ballgame altogether; we have three in this book, all with their own nuances. These wines can be paired with the richest dishes owing to their concentration of fruit, acidity and brilliant nature.

DAVY ŻYW WITH CYRIL BRUN, *CHEF DE CAVE* AT CHARLES HEIDSIECK

The 101

★

There are 101 champagnes and sparkling wines in this book; the 51 champagnes are my favourites and many are significant to champagne's success. The other 50 are sparkling wines I have found through my travels, or on the grapevine – they will surprise, impress and I hope inspire you to drink differently. I have discovered these beauties in the course of my last thirteen years in the wine industry, and have painstakingly tasted each and every bottle.

While this is an ice-bucket list of champagnes to try, no list is definitive and I recognise that everyone has their own preferences when it comes to their favourite fizzer. However, I can, hand on heart, say the bubble-filled bottles in these pages will rock your socks off. I promise that it's worth saving those pennies and every so often cashing them in for a bottle or two of the world's greatest drink.

PRICE

Champagne is expensive! It is part of the allure. But, in the wider scheme of things, it is well priced compared with some wines. Lots of people get the wrong end of the stick when it comes to the value of a wine. Fine wines can be priced at £1,000 a bottle (at least!) because of simple economics: supply vs demand.

If a bottle of wine retails at more than £30, it means there are factors other than purely production costs which make it more expensive. The same can generally be said for champagnes over £50. Considering champagne is one of the most desirable wines in the world, it is arguably good value, given that the most expensive bottles retail at only a few hundred pounds rather than thousands. But with increasing consumer demand, prices of champagne and other fine sparkling wines are only going up.

Most, but not all, of the champagnes I have included here won't sell for much under £20, although you will find some under £10. Champagnes are often heavily discounted by retailers, especially over the festive period. Making sparkling wine is time consuming and expensive, but we have alternative, cheaper options available: crémant, lambrusco, cava, moscato and prosecco to name a few, all featured in this book.

Although discounts and prices may vary, I have based my pricing codes on the following:

£	*Under £10*
££	*Under £30*
£££	*Between £30 and £50*
££££	*Between £50 and £100*
£££££	*Over £100*

THE FACTORS THAT MAKE SPARKLING WINE TASTE THE WAY IT DOES

Vineyard

Where the vines are grown directly affects the flavour of the grapes, resulting in different expressions in your glass. Soils, altitude and exposure to the elements and sun affect the ripening and quality of grapes, and ultimately the finished champagne or wine. In Champagne, the best-quality vineyards are classified as Grand Cru or Premier Cru, which generally indicates a higher level of chalk, resulting in the best-quality champagnes. Chalk is champagne's calling card; its good drainage and mineral character mean grapes can reach full ripeness of sugar and flavour, while retaining high acidity and low pH. Many of the world's best vineyards have either chalk or calcareous elements, giving the wines purity and minerality. This character translates into wines with full flavour while retaining great freshness and longevity.

Another important factor in finished quality is the yield at harvest. As a rule of thumb, the smaller the yield at harvest, the more concentration and flavour in the finished wine. Organic and biodynamic vineyards produce smaller yields, and produce the most flavoursome grapes; I have included a few of these in the following pages. I love wines that taste of where they are from; this taste of somewhereness is what the French call *terroir*.

Vintage

Grapes should only be produced once a year. Many factors throughout an annual growing cycle affect the vine and final quality of the grapes picked at harvest. Vintage variation is particularly relevant in cool climate regions like Champagne, or England. If it is a particularly hot year the grapes will be riper, have sweeter flavours and less acidity; in a cool year, the wines will have higher acid and more tart fruit flavours.

By blending multiple vintages together, champagne houses can produce consistent styles year after year to maintain house style and consistency of quality. As these styles make up the lion's share of any champagne house's production, it is important for houses to create the best champagne at this level. Prosecco and cava are similar as they don't often declare vintages and tend to be a blend of a few years of harvests.

When a vintage is declared on the label, it is a celebration of a specific year, and is generally produced only in good or great years. Only 6% of all champagne production is a vintage product, a tiny proportion considering all other fine wine regions in the world declare and celebrate a vintage every year, in good and bad years. I think we will be seeing more and more vintage champagnes and sparkling wines being produced, with climate change producing more regular vintages.

Vinification (wine making)

Vinification (how a wine is made) is a fundamental factor in the way the finished sparkling wine will taste. Although all champagne is made by the *méthode traditionnelle* (MT) there are many possible ways to do it. Whether the wine was handled oxidatively or reductively (without oxygen); whether fermentation was quick and controlled or wild and slow, giving more complex flavours; what type of press or storage vessel was used – steel, wood barrel or cement: these all have an influence on the final taste. Reserve wines for MT sparkling wines are a house's secret weapon, and how they use, age and mature their reserve wines drastically affects the flavour of what's in your glass. Reserve wines can be aged in oak, steel or even in bottle and can be up to 20 or 30 years old by the time they are blended into the new champagne, giving more texture and complexity of flavour.

For tank-method sparkling wines, such as prosecco, the fermentation is cold and quick, retaining the most pure flavours of the fruity grapes in the final wine. There are thousands of ways to vinify wines and make sparkling; knowing how best to manipulate these techniques to produce the best wines is the responsibility of the head winemaker (*chef de cave*).

Blend of grapes

The grape used to make a wine plays a fundamental role in how a wine and fizz will taste. Each grape variety (there are thousands) has its own unique character and flavour, vigour and style. This is before we get into different clonal selection or genetic properties of particular vines.

Champagne can be made with six grape varieties grown in the region. But three grapes – red grapes pinot noir, pinot meunier and white grape chardonnay – are by far the most important, each making up a third of the region's planting. Each grape carries a different flavour, and the proportions used will create a different expression. Blends of the three grapes are the most common, but blanc de blancs made from white grapes and blanc de noirs made exclusively from red grapes are also important. Most of the world's best sparkling wines mirror the grapes used in Champagne, particularly chardonnay as it is very versatile and grows well in most places. The grapes used in prosecco give a very different style of wine, simpler, with more flavour; the grapes in cava are different again.

Time

Champagne is bottled time. Each non-vintage style has a minimum of 15 months' ageing on lees (deposits of residual yeast), but often a lot longer, meaning the youngest champagne on shelf will be two years old. Vintage champagne has a minimum of 36 months before release, while prestige cuvées often have up to six years' ageing. Generally, the older champagnes will have more toast and nutty flavours, the younger fresher and fruitier ones. Normally the older the wine, the more secondary or tertiary flavours you find, deriving from the evolution of the fruity flavours of the grapes. If you have ever tasted a wine which has been forgotten at the back of the cupboard for many years, you will know how to spot these 'mature' flavours. Prosecco can be made in 60 days from harvest, so the flavours are fresh, fruity and primary.

Sweetness
Most sparkling wines are labelled with a sweetness level: brut, extra brut, demi-sec, doux, etc. 90% of all champagne is made in a brut style, which translates to less than a gram of sugar in your glass. These drier styles of sparkling are by far the most popular, but prosecco's rise in popularity is because it does taste a little sweet. In fact, the most popular champers and prosecco have almost identical sweetness but because of prosecco's lower acid it is easier to drink. Prosecco is usually labelled as brut or extra dry; confusingly 'extra dry' is actually sweeter than brut.

Style
This is the *je ne sais quoi* . . . the X factor. Each champagne or sparkling wine producer has their own house style. Many house or producer styles have been honed and whittled over hundreds of years. Both history and the *chef de cave* dictate the style they make each year, and many *chefs* will follow a similar recipe every year to achieve consistency.

The best houses have their own unique approach, which both separates them from the competition and links the champagnes they produce. The styles of many sparkling wines are more generic, not in an unpleasant way but because the producer has a different philosophy. For commodity wines like prosecco, uniformity is no bad thing.

★

★

THE CHAMPAGNES

★

Understanding the champagne label

★

Here are the basics of what to expect. Note that champagne styles mix the various categories below, i.e. a champagne can be blanc de blancs, vintage and brut.

GRAPES

Doesn't say? It is most likely to be a blend of the three main grape varieties of champagne: chardonnay, pinot noir and pinot meunier. There are seven grapes permitted but the forgotten four are rarely used: pinot gris, pinot blanc, petit meslier and arbane.

Blanc de blancs, white champagne: 100% chardonnay, a white grape. Literally a white wine from white grapes, these styles are often fresher, lighter and more lemony than other champagne styles. If aged, they tend to be toastier. Can be multi-vintage or vintage.

Blanc de noirs, white champagne: Odd, I know, a white wine from red grapes. Blanc de noirs is 100% from black grapes, pinot noir or pinot meunier, or a blend of the two. This style tends to be fuller in the mouth, rounder and shows more red apple and red berry character. Can be multi-vintage or vintage.

Rosé, pink champagne: pink champagne can be made in two ways: leaving the juice in contact with the black skins of pinot noir and/or meunier to extract colour and flavour; blending red wine with clear to produce the desired style and colour. All grape juice is clear when pressed, so the colour comes from the skins. Can be a blend of any of the champagne grapes including a red grape.

VINTAGE

Non-vintage, NV (multi-vintage): By far the most popular and widely available of all champagne styles, accounting for 90% of all production. These tend to the starting point in all champagne ranges, but you can find some premium examples. Often annoyingly referred to as NV: this isn't non-vintage but a blend of multiple vintages.

Vintage: Vintage champagne must contain the wine of a single harvest, and is only made in the best of years. Champagne houses on average produce vintage champagnes in only six years out of ten. Can be a blend of grapes or blanc de noirs or blanc de blancs. Often the most expensive and desirable.

SWEETNESS LEVELS

Brut nature / Zero dosage / Ultra brut: 0–2.5g sugar per bottle. Razor sharp, bone dry. Rare, generally made by producers who want to showcase the flavour and style of the fruit and *terroir*. Can age very well.

Extra brut: 0–4.5g sugar per bottle. Dry. Generally made by quality-focused producers; these are some of my personal favourites.

Brut: 0–9g sugar per bottle. By far the most popular style of champagne and made by most producers. A touch of sweetness in every glass.

Extra sec / Extra dry: 9–13g sugar per bottle. Rare, off-dry style which most producers will just label as brut.

Sec: 13–24g sugar per bottle. Medium-sweet style, a rarity, delicious with cheese.

Demi-sec: 24–37.5g sugar per bottle. Perfect for puddings – sweet, fizzy, delicious.

Doux: >37.5g sugar per bottle. Very rare, very sweet. A nod to the original champagne style, can taste like cream soda and lemonade.

CLASSIFICATION

Champagne is the largest wine region with a single appellation (legally defined growing region) in France. Within this appellation, there are two important classifications of vineyard.

Grand Cru: the best class; just 17 of 319 listed villages in the region have this status. These wines are the most sought after for blending components, as they tend to be the most flavoursome and long-lasting. They have more *terroir* character and shelf-life.

Premier Cru: the second best class; 42 of the 319 listed villages have this status. Some of these wines are of parallel quality to their Grand Cru partners, and will be better priced because of it.

The Rest: champagnes that don't carry Grand or Premier Cru status are not of substandard quality; rather they fall outside the original classification. The rules are hundreds of years old and almost irrelevant these days. For example, Dom Pérignon is sourced predominantly from Grand Cru vineyards, but Premier Cru makes up a small percentage, so legally Dom Pérignon cannot be labelled as Grand Cru. It's all or nothing.

MÉTHODE TRADITIONNELLE

Making champagne and sparkling wine from this method
is the most complex, expensive and time-consuming way
to produce wine. It requires a huge amount of skill and
understanding of a region's soils, weather, vintages, grape
varieties, vineyards and complex production methods
alongside the science of fermentation and manipulation of
time itself.

This method is complex whether you make a hundred
or a million bottles, and I have huge respect for the
larger producers, whose quality and consistency are often
overlooked. As Pierre Casenave of Veuve Clicquot explained to
me: After the base wine is created and before the base wine is
put into the bottle (for the start of the *méthode traditionnelle*)
a *chef de cave* (head winemaker) may blend 30,000 different
wines from different vineyards, areas, grapes varieties and
different years (with diverse complexities of each vintage),
to produce a consistent quality-driven wine. This not only
showcases the house style, but the vintage and even the
personality of the *chef de cave*. This is why, whether you drink
Veuve Clicquot today or in 50 years' time, you know that the
distinctive orange label guarantees a certain style. Although
the champagne will not be made from the same vineyards,
wine or year, it will be a definitive showcase of the house style,
expressing not only the winemaker's signature, but providing
a glimpse into the personality of the Widow Clicquot herself.
Chapeau!

The evolution of techniques has taken hundreds of years to
refine and perfect which results in the ultimate expression we
now find in our champagne and wine glasses today.

★

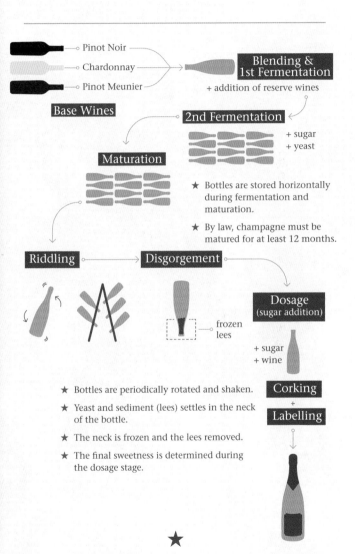

Pinot Noir
Chardonnay
Pinot Meunier

Base Wines

Blending & 1st Fermentation
+ addition of reserve wines

2nd Fermentation
+ sugar
+ yeast

Maturation

★ Bottles are stored horizontally during fermentation and maturation.

★ By law, champagne must be matured for at least 12 months.

Riddling → Disgorgement

frozen lees

Dosage (sugar addition)
+ sugar
+ wine

Corking + Labelling

★ Bottles are periodically rotated and shaken.

★ Yeast and sediment (lees) settles in the neck of the bottle.

★ The neck is frozen and the lees removed.

★ The final sweetness is determined during the dosage stage.

★

Type: Champagne, brut, multi-vintage
Style: Electric Stone fruit
Price: £££
Stockists: Specialist
Toast:
Food: Mum's fish pie
Occasion: Leaving drinks (and you're glad they're leaving)
Website: www.champagne-agrapart.com

Tasting note: *White flowers, apricots, marzipan, Wagon Wheels
and touch of runny honey on the nose. Nectarine flesh, yellow, ripe
and dripping with flavour, green-apple crunch, touch of funk and
bay leaf. Energetic mousse dances on an electric fence of vivid chalky
minerality. A real banger.*

1*

AGRAPART ET FILS LES 7 CRUS

FEW PEOPLE IN CHAMPAGNE CAN CLAIM TO BE FOURTH-GENERATION farmers of the same vines. Pascal and brother Fabrice's family have been cultivating their prime-time vineyards since 1894. Although their roots are deeply bedded in their chalk foundations their outlook is very much above the horizon and their styles are right on trend with the moving times. Agrapart are regarded as one of the best producers on the Côtes des Blancs – a big claim but no one is going to argue with it.

They are on the cusp of organics/ biodynamics, but don't want to be restricted by bureaucratic certification, so go with the flow. Their emphasis is on the farming of their vines and expressing their *terroir* (sense of place); all fermentations are natural as Agrapart feel this is necessary to fully express the land. Although new wood is avoided, old oak barrels are a mainstay in the Agrapart winery. The wines are always bottled at the time of a full moon, a nod to the ancient principles of biodynamics.

The Agrapart range is extensive and brilliant, but nothing is better value than their multi-vintage Les 7 Crus. The name refers to the seven village crus from where it is sourced: home town Avize then Cramant, Oger, Oiry, Avenay Val d'Or, Bergères-les-Vertus and Mardeuil. A blend of 90% chardonnay and 10% pinot noir, this champagne is always based on two harvests, currently from 2015 and 2014. It is aged in oak barrels, then rested on lees for 32 months before disgorgement. Low sugar, at just over 5 grams of sugar per bottle, this is a balancing mix of *terroir*, rich maturation flavours and vivid chalky freshness. Outstanding value!

Type: Champagne, blanc de noirs, multi-vintage
Style: Fizzing eccentric complexity
Price: £££
Stockists: Specialists
Toast:
Food: Roast ham with cola glaze and spiced lentils, or some funky cheese
Occasion: Forgetting Brexit
Website: n/a

Tasting note: *Complex, wine-like and ludicrously attractive. Pruney too with burnt apple crumble and vanilla custard on the nose. A delicious touch of funk, with a wild honey and waxy edge to the palate framed by waves of golden-apple flavours, jasmine and tropical fruit. Delicious, creamy mousse, silky but pretty serious, super-mineral and chalky which takes the flavours on and on in the mouth . . . ending with a marmite-on-toast intensity.*

2 *

ANDRÉ CLOUET UN JOUR DE 1911

CURRENT PROPRIETOR JEAN-FRANÇOIS MAKES HIS WINES IN THE heartland of Champagne's most prized pinot noir vineyards around the Grand Cru village of Bouzy. His family have been guardians of these vines since the 1400s and making wine since the time Dom Pérignon was trying to figure out how to get started. The elaborate, fabulous labels were designed by his great-grandfather in 1911, a nod to the family's printing firm, which used to print books for the French kings. But despite this richly textured history the wines are at the forefront of modern champagne and drip with personality. Respect for the pure chalk vineyards is key for Jean-François, and his wines are a reflection of the incredible *terroir* in which his pinot noir grows. Considering the styles, unbelievable quality and value in all of André Clouet's wines, I imagine when the rest of the world gets a whiff, these champagnes will become collectors' items.

This is a multi-vintage expression of Jean-François's top selection of his best plots in Bouzy. It is a blend of vintages, 50% of which are from the epic vintage of 2002, and the other half from reserve wines which Jean-François keeps in a solera system: a method of fractional blending to gain complexity, similar to the way the Andalusians make sherry. The 2002 component was fermented in barrels of sauternes, which is a sweet wine from Bordeaux. This gives an incredible depth of flavour and preserved sweetness to the blend. Only 1911 bottles per year are ever produced of this exceptional champagne, and it could sell for four times its price. It gives ANY top prestige cuvée a run for its money, so get online and buy some, before I do.

Type: Champagne, brut, blanc de noirs, vintage
Style: Strawberries dipped in a white chocolate fountain
Price: ££££
Stockists: Specialist
Toast:
Food: Monkfish with saffron, or mushroom risotto
Occasion: Summer solstice
Website: http://champagne-arlenoble.com

Tasting note: *Generous and intense red cherry, white pepper dance on the mousse with punnets of wild strawberries bursting on the palate. This is a special style of champagne, unique to the pinot vines of Bisseuil which boogie with the oak flavours of cocoa and vanilla, giving a perceived sweetness, although sugar is at 3 grams per bottle so it is very dry. The freshness is grapefruit and salty, carrying the flavours on with a chalky salinity. When you get round to popping this beauty open, don't serve it too chilled as you'll mask its lavishness (and don't drink it out of bloody flutes).*

3*

AR LENOBLE PREMIER CRU BLANC DE NOIRS BISSEUIL 2012

BASED IN DAMERY IN THE HEARTLAND OF THE VALLÉE DE LA MARNE, brother Antoine and sister Anne Malassagne continue the family tradition, begun in the 1920s, of making creative and expressive styles to rival any in Champagne. Over the years, the philosophy may have changed, but the unfaltering search for quality has never been quenched.

They farm the vines almost organically, nurturing as much healthy biodiversity in the vineyards as possible. Adapting their approach to best suit the vintage they constantly experiment to get the best style and expression from their vines. Considering the small scale of the operation and quality, AR Lenoble could be charging a lot more for their champagnes. For me they are in a select forward-thinking group who are making some of the most exciting wines in Champagne right now. In 2018 Anne launched the 'Mag 14' concept, which has been in development for almost ten years. Lenoble are now keeping their reserve wines in magnum, under cork, to boost complexity and, importantly, freshness. This is the first producer I have found who is adapting their reserve wines to counter the recent warmer vintages due to climate change. I expect a lot of houses to follow in their footsteps.

Made exclusively from pinot noir, over a third of the blend has been vinified and aged in oak barrels. This technique gives a more wine-like character to the finished champagne; the oxygen which slowly percolates through the oak softens the textures of the wine and gives flavours of roasted coffee and vanilla. This style of champagne needs a little time to show its true colours. I would recommend cellaring for a couple of years to show this wine's potential.

Type: Champagne, brut, multi-vintage
Style: Gold-plated peaches and cream
Price: £££££
Stockists: High street
Toast: 🍞🍞🍞🍞
Food: Caviar on your yacht
Occasion: YOLO
Website: http://armanddebrignac.com

Tasting note: *Golden and foaming in your glass, this champers is super-creamy and toasty, positively booming with roasted pineapple and vanilla ice cream with caramel glaze. The palate is peaches and cream, cherry, golden apple, cinnamon and nutmeg spices, brioche and lemon meringue pie; it's sexy and supple. Long finish, touch of oatmeal from the chardonnay with a sprinkle of salinity. Totally over the top.*

4★

ARMAND DE BRIGNAC BRUT GOLD 'ACE OF SPADES'

WHEN SHAWN 'JAY Z' CARTER BOUGHT ARMAND DE BRIGNAC Champagne in 2014 (having made the owners an offer they 'simply couldn't refuse'), the Ace of Spades champagne became the number one choice of champagne, to the rapper's delight. This purchase was in retaliation after the CEO of Louis Roederer, who make Jay Z's old fav' tipple Cristal, publicly announced he did not want any further endorsements from the rap star, as it was ruining Cristal's image. A brave move: Jay Z got even by buying his other choice champagne house. Ace of Spades was first endorsed by Jay Z in 2006 when the blingin' bottle appeared in his music video *Show Me What You Got*. Ever since it has been the choice tipple of gangsters, Wall Street bankers, celebrities and wannabes. You've got to admit, it looks the part!

Fancy bars and restaurants are where you drive desirability and brand visibility. This is a champagne which was created for that market, and it's done beautifully well. The champagne style is immediate and rich, perfect for a Manhattan rooftop or on a yacht in Saint-Tropez. The clever-marketing, way-over-the-top bottle looks banging in your ice bucket. This champagne is the epitome of the glamorous and ostentatious lifestyle with which champagne is often associated, but which only a select few get to live.

It is a blend of three vintages, currently 2009, 2010 and 2012, and the three main champagne grapes chardonnay, pinot noir and pinot meunier, with a big dollop from Grand Cru vineyards. This champagne isn't for everyone: you are paying for packaging and branding of course. But the quality will deliver to novices and champagne connoisseurs alike.

Type: Champagne, brut, multi-vintage
Style: An authority of quality
Price: £££
Stockists: Berry Bros. & Rudd (BBR)
Toast: 🍞🍞🍞
Food: Deep-fried haggis or risotto primavera
Occasion: Landing your dream job
Website: https://www.bbr.com

Tasting note: *All the hallmarks of a topper champagne, with buttered brioche, floral hits, apricots dried and fresh, and beautiful gingerbread flavours. The palate is seamless spade of foaming fizz, golden fruit flavour and firm, Grand Cru minerality on the finish leaving you gasping for another glass.*

5*

BERRY BROS. & RUDD 'UKC' CHAMPAGNE BRUT

FOUNDED IN 1698, BERRY BROS. & RUDD ARE THE WORLD AUTHORITY on wine quality and storytelling. Although the historical ledgers have been lost in the mists of time, the family-owned company believe they are in fact the oldest wine merchant in the world – and by far the most celebrated. And I'm not just saying that because I work there!

Based in the historical cellars in St James in central London, the company has been providing fine wines to the world's richest and most discerning wine drinkers for centuries, but has redefined itself in recent years. Berrys only work with the best wineries from around the world.

Champagne producer Mailly, from the Grand Cru village of the same name, is the only champagne house to work exclusively with Grand Cru vineyards. The vines are tended by the village's 80 wine growers, all of whom are descendants of the handful of men who established and realised the potential of the Mailly *terroir* generations earlier. The chalk-rich soils provide excellent wines with minerality and longevity which makes the wines from here so desirable to all the *chefs de caves* in Champagne. The vineyards are in the heart of the Montagne de Reims: the pinot noir from the north-facing slopes is their golden ticket, and wines crafted from these single vineyards give a fresh fruit character like nowhere else in Champagne.

The Berry Bros. & Rudd 'UKC' Champagne has earned a place at the table with the best champagnes available in the UK. The multi-vintage selection is a blend of 75% pinot noir and 25% chardonnay for salinity and longevity. This Grand Cru blend spent three years resting peacefully in the Mailly cellars before release, and is sold exclusively via BBR.

Type: Champagne, brut, multi-vintage
Style: Harmonic fizzy luminosity
Price: £££
Stockists: High street
Toast: 🍞🍞🍞
Food: Good enough to drink on its own, but chicken thighs roasted with lemons and shallots would go down a treat
Occasion: FriYAY
Website: www. champagne-billecart.fr

Tasting note: *Complex and layered in style with dangerous drinkability. Fruits of red apple, white cherry, and juicy William pears. Fruit and freshness are arranged perfectly with air-light panna-cotta creaminess and mineral, chalky elegance.*

6*

BILLECART-SALMON BRUT RÉSERVE

THERE ARE FEW CHAMPAGNE HOUSES WHICH LIVE UP TO THE MODEST brilliance of Billecart-Salmon. For this family-run producer everything is done to exacting standards for the last 200 years. The current owners Antoine and François are sixth generation; they taste every day at 11:30 with their father Jean Roland-Billecart. Already in his mid 90s, he has over 75 vintages of experience! He is still the boss in the blending room and constantly challenges the young guns on their blends. Quality is paramount to this house, and, unlike a few of its competitors, advertising and marketing campaigns are at the bottom of the priority list.

The house of Billecart-Salmon is intertwined with the small town of Mareuil-sur-Ay, connected by chalk cellars beneath the boulevards. Billecart's production is small compared with the amount of wine they vinify each year. They only accept the crème de la crème and sell off the selection they do not think are worthy. You will undoubtedly be drinking B class Billecart when you drink some of the other more famous branded champagnes.

The Brut Réserve is a blend of the three different champagne grapes, including one of the largest proportions of pinot meunier for a Grande Marque, at close to 40%. The balance of the blend is from the regal grapes of pinot noir and chardonnay, the majority from Billecart's best Grand Cru vineyards. Reserve wines play a major role in this wine's brilliance: over a third of the blend comes from reserve wines, a mixture of older vintages and lightly oaked wines, which pump extra richness and depth of flavour on the palate. Longer cellaring of at least three years, in the belly of Billecart's cellars until the time is right for release, means this wine reaches us at the optimum time to enjoy.

Type: Champagne rosé, brut, multi-vintage
Style: Pink romantic prowess
Price: £££
Stockists: Specialist
Toast:
Food: Sushi
Occasion: Valentine's, baby!
Website: www.champagne-billecart.fr

Tasting note: *A bouquet of cherry blossom, plums and red fruit hail from the glass. This iconic rosé is light and elegant in style, super mineral, vivid cherry and blood oranges. It can be confused with a white champagne when tasted blind, even for the more experienced tasters. Long and precise with freshness and raspberry charm, this champagne is dangerously moreish and definitely an aphrodisiac.*

7*

BILLECART-SALMON BRUT ROSÉ

IF YOU ARE LUCKY ENOUGH TO VISIT THE WINERY, YOU WILL NOTICE it's clinically spankers, which already evokes the clean and correct wine styles of the house. In 1952 Billecart was the first to pioneer cold settling of the grape before fermentation, a technique which is now used all over Champagne, giving clarity and fruitiness to the final wine style. This process was years ahead of its time, and the inspiration came from a family member who brewed beer. After the grapes are cold, they go into the first fermentation; keeping the grapes cool protects their fruity and fresh flavours, but also gains complexity of flavour. Most champagne houses would ferment for ten days, Billecart-Salmon need thirty. This technique is expensive and time consuming, but for Billecart only the best is good enough.

Over the years Billecart-Salmon has forged a reputation as the go-to champagne for *sommeliers* and connoisseurs. This is due to its understated presence in the market, but more importantly to the clever and cleansing wine styles it produces. Fruit, freshness and acidity are the house's signature, and *sommeliers* often gravitate to higher-acid wines which cleanse their palates (they might be tasting hundreds of wines every service). Acidity is a vital pillar in all wines, and it is often this quality which makes wines such versatile food companions.

Billecart-Salmon's brut rosé has become one of the most famous rosés in the world, let alone Champagne. A splash of 7% red pinot noir in the blend gives this wine its delicate salmon-pink hue, and elegant yet vivid red-fruit character. This champagne tastes best in its youth, so if you are lucky enough to chance a bottle, grab your lover and drink it together.

Type: Champagne, brut, vintage
Style: The best of the best
Price: £££
Stockists: High street
Toast:
Food: Injera with chickpea masala
Occasion: Hogmanay
Website: www.champagne-bollinger.com

Tasting note: *Brioche with raisins and candied fruit flavours foam together with crème pâtissière. Bright fresh fruits, red apples and orange peel play on the palate with lemon curd on buttered toast. Complex rich and round, mega!*

8*

BOLLINGER GRANDE ANNÉE 2007

BOLLINGER'S HOUSE CHARACTER IS UNAPOLOGETICALLY STYLISH, appealing to discerning and new champagne lovers alike. For a house with such market presence on the high street, Bollinger's quality and brand is in a league of its own. What better champagne to represent Queen and Country?

Bollinger is the only house to have its own cooper, a skilled craftsman whose sole purpose is to make and re-work oak barrels. I've seen the results of his work: cellars containing 3,500 polished, grained oak barrels which smell incredibly woody, sweet and perfumed. Never made from new; some are over 100 years old, bought from their sister winery Chanson in Burgundy. Using older oak barrels means the flavour imparted by the wood is very subtle, giving light oxidation which translates to richness and golden flavour in the finished champagnes.

Bollinger release 3 million bottles a year but, under the winery, resting peacefully on cork in the dark, are 12 million bottles of reserve champagne. This is what sets Bollinger apart: these could be sold as champagne, but *chef de cave* Giles opens each bottle by hand and blends them back into the champagnes he does release. This adds a unique complexity and toasty richness to the wines, just as double-cooked chips are even more delicious than their single counterparts.

This is Bollinger's celebration of a singular year, sourced from 91% Grand Cru vineyards. It is pinot dominant with most of the fruit from the hills behind the Bollingers' house. 2007 was a varied year in Champagne, but Bollinger nailed it: this is delicious and confidently fresh. Made in oak barrels, followed by eight years resting quietly under the house, this champagne is ready to pop now, or can be cellared until past 2025 no problem.

Type: Champagne, brut, multi-vintage
Style: Glazed golden eye
Price: ££
Stockists: High street
Toast:
Food: Roasted pork loin with pancetta, apples and figs, or cheesy kettle-chips
Occasion: *Skyfall* is on the telly
Website: www.champagne-bollinger.com

Tasting note: *Russet apple and dried figs, pine kernels, toffee apples and beeswax lead into floral highlights, camomile and tea. Foaming and soft, with bags of crunchy red apple bite, creaming with the charred edges of a pecan pie.*

'I drink it when I'm happy and when I'm sad. Sometimes I drink it when I'm alone. When I have company I consider it obligatory. I trifle with it if I'm not hungry and drink it when I am. Otherwise I never touch it – unless I'm thirsty.'
LILY BOLLINGER, DAILY MAIL, 1961

9 *

BOLLINGER SPECIAL CUVEÉ

When Madame Lily Bollinger took up the reins in 1941, Bollinger realised its full potential. Aged 42, the Scots woman had lost her husband in the Second World War and took control of the family firm with passion and vision. At the time it was very unusual to have a woman in such a high position in business, and it was her leadership that propelled Bollinger and wider champagne on the trajectory of success it still enjoys. Her no-nonsense approach is still felt at the house today, but it's her charm and warmth you can taste in the wines.

It's a relatively small house considering its popularity, but has made up for it in quality and craftsmanship; it is one of the last two Grandes Marques which are still independently owned. Centred in the town of Ay, home of the best pinot noir in the region, it produces the best results in your glass.

Bollinger first appeared in Ian Fleming's *Diamonds are Forever* in 1956, as Her Majesty's Secret Service could only choose the most 'British' of champagnes. Note the Royal Warrant on every bottle, granted in 1884 by Queen Victoria; this royal relationship still thrives today.

Few brut multi-vintages are as delicious as Bollinger's. The blend is pinot dominant, with a dash of chardonnay and a seasoning of meunier crafted from over 240 different components from Premier and Grand Cru vineyards. It has partial vinification in oak casks, giving weight and complexity, then customised with Bollinger's secret weapon – reserve wines from magnum bottles of champagnes, giving more flavour, more champagne quality and more identity, which fit together like a tailored tux.

Type: Champagne, ultra brut, vintage
Style: Creamy dream
Price: £££££
Stockists: Specialist
Toast: 🍞🍞🍞🍞
Food: Hens' teeth
Occasion: Trump's impeachment
Website: www.champagnebrunopaillard.com/en

Tasting note: *Super-vinous like a well-cellared, sparkling fine burgundy. Mind-boggling richness and complexity with layers of enveloping flavour of candied fruits, macchiato, savoury spices underpinned by mineral salinity which makes your mouth yearn for another sip. Washed with smooth, golden effervescence and filled with remarkable toasty flavours of crème caramel, fresh baguette and tarte au citron.*

10*

BRUNO PAILLARD N.P.U. 2002

BORN IN THE CAPITAL OF CHAMPAGNE, REIMS, BRUNO PAILLARD can trace his family of Grand Cru vine growers back to 1704. In 1981, at the ripe age of 27 years young, he sold his car, a collectable old Jaguar no less, and put every penny into his own new venture.

Fast forward and Bruno Paillard is producing some amazing, creative champagnes. Although they aren't as easy to find as those from some more famous houses, you will be rewarded if you invest time in finding these wines. A great champagne for Bruno Paillard is all about purity and smooth effervescence; he never adds more than 3 grams of sugar to his wines, keeping his styles pure and fresh. He cellars his champagnes longer than most, but there is one special champagne which stays longer in his cellars than any other: his prestige cuvée N.P.U. (Nec Plus Ultra).

N.P.U. 2002 has spent 15 years in Bruno's cellars before release, and a whacking 11 years on lees developing incredible complexity and toastiness. Bruno is one of the last quality producers to release the 2002 vintage, a stonker year in champagne; for example Dom Pérignon launched their 02 in 2010.

A blend of 50% chardonnay and 50% pinot noir from six Grand Cru villages. Entirely fermented in oak barrels, this is an unashamedly deep style of champagne. It was disgorged in September 2014 to let the wine relax and integrate before release. Bruno compares disgorgement to someone in recovery from an operation: the more time the better.

Only 6,200 bottles have been produced of this wine, all individually numbered. This is a champagne of the highest quality, and I respect the bottled time which the N.P.U. represents. Nec Plus Ultra is Latin for 'Nothing further beyond'. If this was the last champagne I ever drank, I'd be very happy.

Type: Champagne, extra brut, vintage
Style: Golden Granny Smith
Price: ££££
Stockists: Specialist
Toast:
Food: Flambé king prawns with cherry tomatoes
Occasion: First (or last!) day of summer hols
Website: www.champagne-cazals.fr

Tasting note: *Perfumed and ripe nose of green apple, white flowers, roasted pineapple and orchard fruit. The palate is Granny Smith with peachy salinity leading into foaming shortbread biscuits and salt-buttered white toast. There is an invigorating sapid, lip-puckering chalky character which adds freshness and length to this stunning example of chardonnay. The depth and deliciousness of this wine foam and linger on the palate and into your mind's eye.*

11*

CHAMPAGNE CLOS CAZALS 2005

FOUNDED IN 1897, THE CAZALS FAMILY HAS A LONG HISTORY OF winemaking, but has only recently started to unlock their unbelievable quality potential. Delphine Cazals is at the helm and is making some radical changes in the Côte des Blancs. The Cazals are sitting on a pot of gold in a field of chalk: the family have some of the best vineyards in the whole region. Historically they have sold most of their grapes to Bollinger and Moët for their top cuvées, but now they are bottling themselves. Delphine is the envy of every single champagne house in the region, as she has the only 'clos' (single, walled vineyard) in her home town of Oger, one of the best vineyard sites in Champagne.

Historically champagne is a blended wine from different vineyards and areas, meaning clos wines are rare, and only made in very small quantities; Cazals only produce a few thousand bottles, and only in the best years. The only other clos wine in the area is made by Krug, who have a single vineyard three minutes' drive away from Delphine's; Krug sell their 'du Mesnil' for almost five times the price of Cazals.

The walled vineyard was planted by Delphine's grandfather in the 1950s beside a small church on the white slopes of the Côte des Blancs. These old vines are rooted directly in the chalk bedrock of the area and produce wines with amazing minerality. The 2005 has a touch of oak barrels giving a spice and roundness to the chalky expression; after ten years resting on lees, this wine has a wonderful toasty character further accentuated by very low sugar of just over 2 grams per bottle. Value isn't often associated with fine champagne, but this truly is bang for buck.

Type: Champagne, brut, multi-vintage
Style: Floral, fruity and fizz
Price: £
Stockists: High street
Toast:
Food: Twiglets or Wotsits
Occasion: Fizz en masse
Website: www.lidl.co.uk

Tasting note: *Champagney, fruity, rather floral and definitely fizzy! On the sweeter side of brut. This has all the champagne cues with mass appeal: apples, pears and a touch of creamy, crumbly biscuits.*

12 *

CHAMPAGNE COMTE DE SENNEVAL

THIS CHAMPAGNE ENTERED THE EUROPEAN MARKET ONLY A FEW YEARS ago, and changed the game of champagne retailing. Champagne is often thought of as an aspiration drink, it holds a prestige, an allure which is helped by the high cost per bottle. This glossy varnish doesn't stick the same when the champagne costs £10 all day every day! I know from my day job that Lidl can't be making money on this champagne, a fractional percentage margin if anything. But the clever retailer knows that having this loss leader will drive a lot of footfall into their stores to buy other items. The wine trade likes to scoff at such wines, but I say bring them on! It might not be the best champagne available, but at £10 a bottle, it's cheaper than a glass of fizz in a bar or restaurant. Thank you to Lidl for passing on the value to the customers, who may have not been able to afford Champagne before and now might want to taste other champagnes in their drinking journey.

Weddings, wakes, office drinks, festive parties, celebrations, whenever you need a fizz to pour willy nilly, value doesn't get better than this for champagne, so stock it up, stack it high and feel free to pour this brut bad boy.

Made for Lidl by cousin company to Lanson champagne houses, the Comte de Senneval comes from good stock. Less time on lees means it doesn't display bags of toasty character, but if you feel the need I would buy a few bottles and stick them away for a year under the stairs. You will be surprised how much richer the champagne becomes after another year of peace and quiet. A traditional blend of all three main champagne grapes – chardonnay, pinot noir and pinot meunier – this is a soft, little sweet, quite floral style of champers, which your dinner guests will knock back with abandon.

Type: Champagne, brut nature, multi-vintage
Style: Pineapple margarita
Price: £££
Stockists: Specialist
Toast: 🍞🍞🍞
Food: Chilli corn dogs with green salsa
Occasion: Liquid brunch
Website: www.champagne-fleury.fr/

Tasting note: *The nose is full of aromatic white flowers, peach and smashed melon on wet stone. The palate is foaming and fleshy, bone dry yet waxy and juicy with flavours of figs, yellow plums, New York cheesecake with candied pineapple, with a steely, salty margarita finish.*

13*

CHAMPAGNE FLEURY NOTES BLANCHES

CHAMPAGNE FLEURY WAS ONE OF THE FIRST BIODYNAMIC PRODUCERS in the whole of Champagne, certified since 1989, paving the way for many growers who have since followed on its coat tails. Based in Aube, in the very south of the Champagne region, the winery is closer to much of Burgundy than most of the northern Champagne region. The winery was originally founded in 1895, and was the first to replant in the area following the phylloxera epidemic. Progression is nothing new for the Fleury family; in 1928 they were the first grower in the Aube to produce and bottle their own champagnes, and the first to make single vintages.

The vineyard is still run by the family, who tend the vines on the chalky slopes on both sides of the Seine valley. The plantings are predominantly pinot noir, famous in the area, but the family also have small holdings of chardonnay and some of the lesser known grapes of Champagne: notably pinot blanc.

All vineyard work is done by hand, including the back-breaking work of ploughing with horses. All grapes are pressed in a traditional basket press and vinified separately, to allow more detailed blending, and ultimately more expression and diversity in the finished wine. These wines are on the 'natural' side, and are testament to the quality achievable with minimal-intervention winemaking.

The Notes Blanches ('white notes') is a quirky act, being an unusual cuvée of 100% pinot blanc, 100% barrel fermented, which gives it weight and character. This grape, which is more associated with the wines of Alsace, gives a fuller, more exotic character to the champagne and needs to be tasted (at least) once in your life!

Type: Champagne, vintage brut, blanc de blancs
Style: Frothing gold ecstasy
Price: £££££
Stockists: Specialist
Toast: ▢▢▢▢▢
Food: Festive fare
Occasion: Your engagement lunch
Website: https://charlesheidsieck.com

Tasting note: *Amazing, pure and racing. A celebration of chardonnay and chalk. This is a champagne built to last and develop in bottle. Loaded with flavour and so lip-smackingly delicious you have to stop everything else you are doing just to appreciate the complexity and the sheer enjoyment of it. Creamy, chalky and flint loaded with honey top notes, salted caramel oatcakes and all-butter shortbread give way to lemon sherbet, gunpowder, toffee apple and razor minerality with waves of fizzing enveloping pleasure.*

14*

CHARLES HEIDSIECK BLANC DES MILLÉNAIRES 2004

THE STAKES HAVE BEEN HIGH: THE LAST RELEASE OF THE LEGENDARY BdM (Blanc des Millénaires) was the 1995 vintage, which I have been lucky to sample on a couple of occasions. I would say it is up there with the best champagnes I've had. The champagne world was on tenterhooks waiting for the next vintage declaration of Charles Heidsieck and new *chef de cave* Cyril Brun's first BdM. Huge pressure. Safe to say they totally nailed it.

The 2004 vintage was a banging year, especially for chardonnay, which makes up the BdM exclusively. The chardonnay came from some of the best vineyards sites in the entire region, all in the Côte des Blancs from the chalk-bedded villages of Vertus, Avize, Cramant, Oger and Le Mesnil-sur-Oger. This champagne can age for 30 years or more, and is one of the most complex, seductive and tantalisingly moreish champagnes anyone is likely to encounter. The unashamedly bold Charles style of champagne is toned down in this BdM in its youth, but the BdM is a ticking time bomb. As the years progress, a different flavour and variant will expose the drinker to the nuances of the different vineyards, the skill of the winemaking and overall complexity. Give this wine time, and its true colours of Charles will be revealed . . .

I had a bottle; I was planning to cellar it for at least 10 years before popping the cork. But it only lasted a couple of months. I got engaged and had to toast with a wine which not only delivers now, but has potential that I can revisit and enjoy in the years and decades to come. If I chance on another bottle, I won't (plan) on drinking it until at least our paper anniversary . . .

Type: Champagne, brut, multi-vintage
Style: The taste of pizzazz
Price: £££
Stockists: High street
Toast:
Food: I would happily drink this on its own, but lobster bisque with croutons, or garlic bread, is a good shout
Occasion: Hump day
Website: https://charlesheidsieck.com/en/

Tasting note: *Funfair toffee apple and golden light on the nose with apricots and Bombay mix. The palate is runaway train of Christmas cake spices, popcorn, Amalfi lemons and charred crumbs of freshly baked butter biscuits. Golden, foaming, mineral and rich.*

15*

CHARLES HEIDSIECK BRUT RÉSERVE

ON MY LAST VISIT TO CHAMPAGNE I ASKED EVERY CHEF DE CAVE I MET which champagnes they drink at home. Charles Heidsieck was by far the most mentioned, the highest endorsement a champagne can have. This wine is their choice, not only because it's bloody delicious, but also because of their respect for the craftsmanship. To make these wines is difficult; it involves a highly technical process of fractional blending of older reserves and younger wines, while maintaining the consistent pizzazz of the house and juggling the demands of the annual market pressures.

This is the entry point to the range but it is by no means an entry-level champagne. It is arguably better quality than many houses' top cuvées. Value isn't often associated with fine wine or champagne, but believe me this champagne is the best bang for buck in the market. For me and many wine critics the only other multi-vintage blend like it is Krug, which is four times the price.

Brut Réserve is multi-vintage champagne, with an equal split of each of the three main champagne grapes, like a lot of other champagnes for sure. But Charles' *pièce de résistance* is their range of reserve wines, of which Brut Réserve make up around 40%. These reserve wines are 10 years old on average but some have components that date back to the 1980s. The Brut Réserve has extended time ageing in the chalk cellars deep under the city of Reims, giving the wines more richness and toastiness.

Sophisticated poise and elegance meet gushing exuberance rarely found in the best of champagnes let alone an 'entry-price' cuvée. The flavour and complexity make you stop what you are doing, envelop yourself in your senses and take notice.

Type: Champagne, blanc de blancs, vintage
Style: Zip-up golden fleece
Price: £££
Stockists: Specialist
Toast:
Food: Turkey sandwiches
Occasion: Bracing Boxing Day walk
Website: www.salondelamotte.com

Tasting note: *Chardonnay for miles, scented with chalk-flaked Braeburn apple, pricked with jasmine and orange blossom. Not in your face, rather subtle and delicate with fine and seamless mousse. The flavours deepen in the mouth with golden fruit and lip-smacking lemons, mineral electric and rather bloody delicious.*

16*

DELAMOTTE CHAMPAGNE BLANC DE BLANCS 2007

CHAMPAGNE'S FIFTH OLDEST HOUSE WAS FOUNDED IN 1760 BY François Delamotte, and has been passed through the family until champagne royalty, the Nonancourt family (owners of Laurent Perrier), took over the reins in the 1980s. LP then took over the running of both Delamotte and Champagne Salon and are in charge of keeping these two iconic champagnes individual and true to their roots. So far so good, even if the winds of change have blown off some of the magic stardust.

Delamotte is essentially the second champagne of Salon, as they both share the same source of vines from the slopes above the town of Le Mesnil-sur-Oger. This is the most prized, and highest priced, Grand Cru village in the Côte des Blancs, where chardonnay thrives on the ancient chalk-rich soils and has become iconic because of quality of champagnes like Delamotte and Salon.

Being the second wine to the most prized blanc de blancs has its drawbacks and its perks. Drawbacks as Delamotte is always in the shadow of its sexier brother. The perks are when the vintage isn't 100% optimum for the style of Salon and they declassify Salon into Delamotte. This means, in a vintage like 2007, you are tasting Salon for a fraction of the price.

Delamotte, like Salon, is an advocate of chardonnay. All the grapes for this blanc de blancs are sourced from the chalkiest of Grand Cru vineyards in the Côte des Blancs. 2007 was a tricky year for some but regarded as good year, especially for chardonnay, which needs time to unravel its spring of tightly wound flavour. After eight years of careful ageing and maturation, the Delamotte Blanc de Blancs is ripe and open for drinking now, or will cellar and develop beautifully for the next 10 to 15 years . . . if you can wait that long.

Type: Champagne, brut, multi-vintage
Style: Class in a glass
Price: ££
Stockists: High street
Toast:
Food: Salmon steaks with miso
Occasion: Fly new haircut
Website: www.champagne-deutz.com

Tasting note: *Smooth and friendly, super-attractive with showcase fresh lemon biscuits and sweet gorse on the nose. Palate is supple, round and dangerously smooth with toasted almonds, citrus and stone fruit style finishing with golden orchard fruit which tantalises the taste buds with flirtatious subtlety.*

17*

DEUTZ BRUT CLASSIC

DEUTZ IS A CHAMPAGNE HOUSE WHICH HAS FORGED ITS REPUTATION on quality and discretion. Established by Germans William Deutz and Pierre-Hubert Geldermann in 1828 in the town of Ay, it remains one of the unsung Grandes Marques, as the quality of their range rivals any of their contemporaries. It remained in family hands until the 1980s when the company was sold to Louis Roederer. The family would only agree to sell to a company who understood their quest for quality, and no one knows integrity like Roederer. There has been huge investment into the winery since then. Production has expanded, which can mean a drop in quality, but here the hallmark of pleasure to price has been maintained. France is by far the biggest market, always an important gauge: the French have a longer relationship with champagne than anyone else.

Deutz is an understated house considering their long history and legacy of pure, elegant champagne styles. I was super-impressed with their entire range, and with increased production at the house we can expect to see more of Champagne Deutz on the shelves and on wine lists.

The Deutz signature is a true essence of elegance and subtlety. The Brut Classic is an equal blend of chardonnay, pinot noir and pinot meunier from Grand and Premier Cru vineyards all over the Champagne region, from Deutz's extensive network of growers on 245 hectares of vineyards. This harmonic style has up to 40% reserve wine blended in for complexity and depth of flavour, but unlike Charles Heidsieck, who use a similar amount, the wines are more restrained than showy. The wine undergoes further ageing for three years in Deutz *berceaux* (cots), where the infant bottles rest in the deep chalk cellars, and are only released when they have reached their prime. This is a multi-vintage brut as good as any – and I like the distinctive bottle shape too.

Type: Champagne, brut, vintage
Style: Better than sex
Price: £££££
Stockists: High street
Toast:
Food: Big Mac, fries and a banana milkshake
Occasion: Someone's death worth celebrating
Website: www.domperignon.com

Tasting note: *Absolutely delicious. Earl Grey tea served in a Boulangerie on Mars. Flavours from another planet, like dried fruits from outer space, you haven't experienced before but just know they are delicious. Smoky, rich, evolving grace, nutty and unbelievably toasty.*

18*

DOM PÉRIGNON P2 2000

As the most iconic champagne, Dom Pérignon has responsibility to the Champagne region and to the DP brotherhood across the world. The DP *chef de cave* job is one of the grandest seats in all winemaking and one of the most contested. There is a change in the guards at Dom Pérignon: legendary Richard Geoffroy, who has been in the hot seat for 28 years, passes the baton to young gun Vincent Chaperon in 2019. Big boots for Vincent to fill: *chapeau!* One of the wines released at the turn of the tide is P2 2000, which I know Richard will cherish in his retirement.

Vintage DP is made only in very good years, always showcasing the uncompromising DP style while keeping faithful to the vintage character. The straight DP vintages spend seven or eight years of ageing before they hit the market. But in exceptional years, selected bottles are held back for limited later release: the P2 stands for 'Plénitude deuxième' or second age. These special bottles are not disgorged, resting on lees for 16 long years. This means the wines evolve slowly, keeping freshness while gaining richness, complexity and to-die-for flavours.

The P2 follows a recent trend in Champagne for later releases of the same wine, so drinkers can enjoy a new experience of a wine they have drunk before. The 2000 release of DP was released again in 2008: the same wine reborn with a multitude of mature aromatics and a timeless energy. The results are stop-what-you-are-doing-and-escape-into-the-galaxy-of-flavour-you-are-experiencing.

This wine is the height of DP's expression, only to be trumped by their P3 which is released after a whopping 30 years. This wine will capture the imagination of the most discerning enthusiasts (with cash to burn!) but also collectors. I recommend drinking soon after purchase for maximum reward – use a proper glass.

Type: Champagne, brut, vintage
Style: The ultimate smooch
Price: ££££
Stockists: High street
Toast:
Food: A lemongrass heavy laksa
Occasion: Opening Dom Pérignon
Website: www.domperignon.com

Tasting note: *Bright and luminous in the glass. Hallmark reductive in style, which translates into an almost smoky, Guy Fawkes Night aroma backed up with upfront candied fruits and salted caramels. Round in the palate, silkier than it is creamy, with notes of toasted nuts, citrus, white peach, chalk and sweet saline with hints of liquorice enveloping the ultimate finish.*

19*

DOM PÉRIGNON VINTAGE 2009

DOM, WHAT ELSE? THE MYTH, THE LEGEND. BELIEVE THE HYPE. DOM Pérignon is the prestige cuvée of Moët & Chandon, part of the goliath luxury brand LVMH. Of all luxury brands of champagne, Dom is the coolest, most famous, the most available, and with good reason: it's bloody delicious.

This wine was created for the UK market in 1935, for its best private customers, over 200 years after the death of the acclaimed monk. It is only declared in the best vintages. My first taste of Dom was when I was 17 and my twin brother threw a surprise party. We were fresh out of catering school and my friend Pete had appropriated a bottle of 1996 Dom from his work. We shot the cork into the street in fits of giggles, but the laughter stopped as soon as I wet my whistle. I didn't know wine or champagne could taste like that.

The production total of DP is a secret guarded as closely as the Holy Grail. I've heard it's anything from 2 to 8 million bottles each release. Big production is often scoffed at, as large volume means diluted quality. With DP this couldn't be further from the truth: the wines are marvellous.

This wine is always a near equal blend of chardonnay and pinot noir, and a celebration of the vintage. 2009 was a sunny year, and you can taste the ripeness of fruit. Like the monk himself, current *chef de cave* Richard Geoffroy has been pushing the boundaries of what champagne is over his 15 declared vintage releases. But unlike Dom, who was looking for divinity through his production, Richard and his successor Vincent Chaperon only want people to appreciate the wines. Next time you see a bottle of DP on the shelf, stick it on the credit card and join the brotherhood.

Type: Champagne, brut, multi-vintage
Style: The oomph of chardonnay
Price: ££££
Stockists: Specialist
Toast: 🍞🍞🍞🍞
Food: Pan roasted John Dory with fondant tatties and greens
Occasion: Conquering your childhood fears
Website: www.ruinart.com

Tasting note: *Pure expression of champagne's top chardonnay, this exquisite blanc de blancs sings with candied citrus fruit, gun powder and glorious, toasted expression. Oatcakes, butterscotch, marmalade and toasted brioche combine with ripe lemons and riveting chalky freshness.*

'*Chardonnay is both the golden thread of Ruinart and also the soul of the House*'–
FRÉDÉRIC PANAIOTIS, CELLAR MASTER

20*

DOM RUINART BLANC DE BLANCS 2006

HAILING FROM THE WORLD'S OLDEST CHAMPAGNE HOUSE, THIS IS A titan of chardonnay. Ever since its first launch in 1966, from the 1959 vintage, this wine has been like gold dust, forging a reputation for some of the highest class of champagne.

There are two famous Doms in Champagne. The underdog is Dom Thierry Ruinart. Legend has it that the two monks were good pals at the Abbey of Hautvillers. If Dom Pérignon was the first man to understand the pressing and blending of champagne, it was Dom Ruinart who began to age champagne properly in the Roman chalk mines in the local capital of Reims. These *crayères* are the perfect place for storing and maturing champagne. The champagne rests and develops underground with no natural light, no vibrations and a yearly constant temperature of around 10°C. Ruinart's chalk cellars are the deepest and most spectacular in the whole of Champagne, tunnelling 38 metres below the streets of Reims, and are the only cellars to be awarded UNESCO World Heritage status.

100% Grand Cru chardonnay, this is one of the most famous expressions of pure chardonnay in Champagne. A mixture of Côte des Blancs for purity, freshness and longevity, blended with fruit from Montagne de Reims, which gives it a more unctuous style of blanc de blancs. It is labelled brut but only carries around 3 grams of sugar in the whole bottle so this is on the drier side. Aged peacefully on lees for ten years before release, it gains wonderful complexity and biscuit character. This champagne is worth robbing a bank for!

Type: Champagne, brut, multi-vintage
Style: Soapy fruit cake
Price: ££
Stockists: High street
Toast: 🍞🍞
Food: Cheesy nachos, or chicken pasties
Occasion: Mother's Day, duh
Website: www.mumm.com/en

Tasting note: *Pale and fizzy. Nose is fruity and slightly floral with a washing-up-liquid edge. On the palate the fruit is foaming, ripe and clean, both lemon pith and zip with some ripe blood orange character, yum-yums and tea cakes.*

21*

G.H.MUMM BRUT

MANY PEOPLE'S FIRST THOUGHT OF CHAMPAGNE IS THE IMAGE OF Formula 1 racers showering each other and the crowd with bubbles of victory with G.H.Mumm Cordon Rouge on the podium. The connection between champagne and racing dates back to the 1950s when the first French Grand Prix was held in Reims, and naturally the winner was presented with a bottle of the good stuff. But this dramatic waste of champagne began, like a lot of the best traditions, totally by accident! At an infamous 24-hour race, Le Mans in 1966, Swiss racer Jo 'Seppi' Siffert accidentally showered the crowd as a bottle of Moët burst open spontaneously after it was left out in the sun. The following year American racer Dan Gurney deliberately copied Seppi's action and so the tradition was born.

This partnership between Mumm and the Grand Prix started in 2000, but came to an end in 2015 when the Mumm's €5 million advertising deal was deemed insufficient. Now you will see Champagne Carbon spraying at $3,000 a bottle over the podium winners from their carbon-plated bottles.

Mumm's champagne story starts in Germany in the 1700s, when Peter Arnold Mumm set up as a wine merchant in his home town of Cologne. The house we know today was set up by his descendants, three winemaking brothers. In 1827 the family set up their own champagne house in Reims. The emblematic Red Ribbon or 'Cordon Rouge' is in homage to the house's most prestigious clients from the Legion of Honour, the highest military order in France, established by Napoleon Bonaparte.

The house is now owned by Pernod Ricard, who have big plans for expansion. The fancy new redesign looks the part, even if the quality has dropped recently. It still offers good value, especially when on discount.

Type: Champagne, brut, multi-vintage
Style: Hand-crafted excellence
Price: £££
Stockists: High street
Toast:
Food: Foie gras and figs glazed with madeira, or a battered black pudding supper
Occasion: Dinner party guests have left, and you can finally enjoy yourself
Website: www.champagne-gosset.com/eng

Tasting note: *Dried fruits, apricots, figs and raisins lift the fragrance with sugar-toasted nuts. The palate is super-fresh, yet richly flavour-filled, unbelievably drinkable with bags of orange zest, green-apple fruit and freshly baked almond croissant character. Explosive, expressive style and dangerously moreish.*

22*

GOSSET GRANDE RÉSERVE BRUT

FAMILY-OWNED GOSSET IS CHAMPAGNE'S OLDEST WINERY, ESTABLISHED in 1584, and has been fine-tuning its wine for over 400 years. Gosset is among the top players of champagne quality yet remains stoically out of the limelight. When your wines are this good there is no need for big marketing budgets. Originally based in Ay, a stone's throw from Bollinger, it moved production and cellars to the epicentre of champagne, Épernay, on Champagne's most prestigious address, Rue de Champagne.

With relatively small production, Gosset is a reflection of handcrafted artisanal champagne in the quest of unfaltering quality over quantity. Like a few other artisanal champagne producers, Gosset tends to avoid malolactic fermentation which means the wines age magnificently well and have a brighter freshness than many other champagnes. These are true gastronomic wines and wouldn't be out of place on any of the top Michelin Star tables.

On my visits to Champagne, I always ask the *chefs de caves* what they like to drink at home, and, other than their own brand and Charles Heidsieck, Gosset was by far the most talked about. My first introduction to Gosset was by the glass when I worked at Le Gavroche, and I always enjoyed steering customers towards this sophisticated champagne, richly textured, immediately enjoyable, and bloody brilliant with food. The Grande Réserve is a blend of the three champagne grapes, with the lion's share of Grand Cru chardonnay. Based on a single vintage with 25% reserve wine from the two older vintages, and aged for four years in the Gosset cellars before release, the result is a delicious toasty richness that retains the mineral signature of the house.

Type: Champagne, extra brut, vintage
Style: Taste like money
Price: ££££
Stockists: Specialist
Toast: 🍞🍞🍞
Food: Chicken and mushroom pie, or spiced lentils, feta and couscous
Occasion: Your accumulator has just come in
Website: www.goutorbe-bouillot.fr

Tasting note: *Fresh and complex nose, Fresh croissant, lemon pith, orange blossom and white flowers, white pepper, black tea and red apple; layered and super complex. The palate is lip-puckering fresh and round, with complex undergrowth; golden fruit and mineral salinity roll through the palate with a wash of mouth-filling foam with steely intensity.*

23*

GOUTORBE-BOUILLOT CLOS DES MONNAIES 2010

CHAMPAGNE GOUTORBE-BOUILLOT'S STARTED IN THE 1750S AND remains fiercely proud of its history and 8 hectares of vines in the Vallée de le Marne. The family motto is 'Nurturing mother earth'; you can expect a bit of a hippy twist to the wines.

Their vineyards, pinot meunier dominant, and their solera system for reserve wines, give the wines a distinctive personality. This method is famed in sherry making, as a way of fractional blending across different years to maintain a consistent style, linking vintages and adding flavour complexity. Barrels of reserve wine may have components in the blend spanning back decades, and it's this balance of mature wines and fresher vintages which gives incredible complexity and depth to the palate.

This special cuvée is from the tiny walled vineyard (clos) in the heart of Damery. The name of 'Clos des Monnaies' was coined after 1840, when the family discovered gold coins in the vineyards; after further excavations it transpired that a Roman coin workshop had been on the very site.

Clos des Monnaies is a blend of 50% pinot meunier and 50% chardonnay, a fairly uncommon blend in champagne. Malolactic fermentation is blocked, keeping a purer style with more *terroir* flavour. The fermentation, and further ageing, take place in neutral oak barrels letting the wines breathe, relax and develop further character. The wines rest patiently on lees for 50 months, gaining toast and richness, then a further year in bottle on cork, before release. With a dose of 3 grams of sugar per bottle, this is a pure and dry style of champagne, an expression of the unique site in Damery and an amazing balance between freshness and maturity. Only 1,282 bottles of the 2010 vintage were produced, so they are as rare as gold coins.

Type: Champagne, brut, multi-vintage
Style: Gluggable goodness
Price: ££
Stockists: High street
Toast:
Food: Cool tortilla chips and dip
Occasion: Work night out
Website: www.heidsieckandco-monopole.com

Tasting note: *Foaming and fiercely fizzy with lemon, ripe orchard fruit and toasted brown bread with butter. The palate is round, pleasing and champagne-like with bags of freshness and sticky apple character.*

24*

HEIDSIECK AND CO. MONOPOLE BLUE TOP

HEIDSIECK & CO. MONOPOLE IS ONE OF CHAMPAGNE'S OLDEST houses, established in 1785 in Epernay. It was the leading brand at the turn of the twentieth century, and its excellent customer list included the King of Prussia, the English courts and Tsar Nicholas II, who had two full trains of bottles sent from Champagne every year for his own consumption. Nowadays it doesn't enjoy such a premium position, and is part of the wider Vranken-Pommery group, but it does offer a range of great value champagnes – none more so than the Blue Top.

The Blue Top is available on our supermarket shelves and is a great all-rounder when champagne is needed. Its history is also linked with the high seas. Heidsieck & Co. was the champagne served on the *Titanic*'s fateful voyage. A few bottles have been salvaged from the watery grave, but have been hoovered up by morbid collectors. In 1916 Heidsieck & Co. sent a shipment of 3,000 bottles to the Russian Army in St Petersburg. It never made it to port, as the *Jönköping* was sunk by a submarine, losing all its crew and its precious cargo. In 1998, a Swedish expedition found the shipwreck, and brought up 2,400 bottles of the 1907 vintage. The cognac and burgundy that had been on board the ship did not survive 82 years in Davy Jones' locker but the bottles of Heidsieck & Co. Monopole seemed to be in perfect condition. The champagne of this time was sweet rather than dry, and supposedly still has a sparkle, as you can discover at £300k a bottle at the Ritz in Moscow!

The newer releases are a bit cheaper. Blue Top is a classic blend of pinot noir, chardonnay and pinot meunier, carefully selected from key regions before ageing in the cellars for up to five years. A commercial style of champers that won't offend anyone looking for a champagne hit.

Type: Champagne, brut nature, multi-vintage
Style: Naturally lean and delightful
Price: £££
Stockists: Specialist
Toast:
Food: Mulligatawny soup with charred cauliflower
Occasion: Close shave with death
Website: www.champagne-giraud.com

Tasting note: *Lively, sherbet lemons and green wine gums on the nose, mixed in with grass cuttings, hay and toasted spices. The palate is foaming with applejack jap, peanuts, with a menthol and nervous green ivy edge. Challenging, razor dry and 100% delicious.*

25*

HENRI GIRAUD ESPRIT NATURE BRUT

CONTEMPORARIES OF HENRI IV, KING OF FRANCE, IN THE 1600S, THE Giraud family settled in Ay at the beginning of the seventeenth century and have never left. The company is now run by twelfth-generation descendant Claude, who has revolutionized his family champagne firm since he took charge in 1983. Claude makes wines which are unapologetically intense, always with the use of oak from the Argonne forest, unique in Champagne today, using fruit from his celebrated Ay Grand Cru vineyard, famous for top-drawer pinot noir.

Small production, sustainable viticulture, barrel fermentation, extended lees ageing, old solera reserve wines, concrete egg-shaped fermentation tanks and terracotta amphora vats, combined, mean the styles from Giraud are some of the most progressive in Champagne today. And with Claude's strong vision and *terroir*-driven styles, the wines are loved by the 'natural' wine movement.

Oak from the Argonne forest, 80km to the east, is the traditional source of wood for Champagne wine production. Claude is the only producer in the region to use the original; he had to obtain specific certification to do so. According to Claude, this was not merely a marketing exercise, but a nod to the original style of champagnes as steel vats only arrived after the war.

Esprit Nature Brut is a blend of 80% pinot noir and 20% chardonnay with a whopping 50% reserve wines from small Argonne barrels with a splash from concrete eggs. I like the artistic label: *le chêne de papier* (the paper oak) symbolises the fragility of life and champagne's origins. There is no great wine without a great forest; this wine celebrates the forest of Argonne, and its importance in the history of champagne.

Type: Champagne rosé, brut, multi-vintage
Style: Rosé tinted glasses
Price: £££££
Stockists: Specialist
Toast:
Food: Thai red curry, or pigeon breast with ceps and raisins
Occasion: Christmas gatherings, but serve your in-laws cava
– this ain't for sharing
Website: www.selosse-lesavises.com

Tasting note: *The nose is layered with waxy fruits, savoury spices and fresh saffron. The palate is wild, showing incredible purity of chalk, lickable salinity supported by tea leaves, dried berries and fresh peaches, browning apple skin and bright red currents. There is a degree of funk to this wine, it shows a little cider note which adds interest and complexity. I love it. The finish is long and memorable – you don't forget this wine in a hurry.*

26*

JACQUES SELOSSE ROSÉ

SELOSSE'S CONTROVERSIAL WINES HAVE KICKSTARTED A HUGE MOVEMENT in Champagne to respect and express the role of *terroir*, and have empowered the voice of the individual grower rather than just the Grandes Marques and bottlers. His biodynamic farming practice manifests itself in the intensity, minerality and flavour of the finished wine. These practices don't stop in the vineyards; the attention and principles of nurturing quality are taken through vinification and winemaking. Anselme Selosse is one of the most respected men in Champagne today, and many of the *chefs de caves* I've met have mentioned him as an example of a man who knows no compromise in the quest of quality and expression, and isn't bothered about chucking out the rule book to do so.

The principles of biodynamics may seem crazy, but many of the best wines are produced following the methods based on the cosmic rhythms of the universe and balance of the farm's ecosystem. These methods involve many ancient practical farming practices including planting and farming in time with lunar cycles, and avoiding any unnatural sprays or pesticides.

Almost painfully *terroir* driven, Selosse's wines aren't easy glugging styles. They need attention and they challenge the drinker, the same way the *terroir* has challenged the Selosse family to make it. This rosé is one of the most sought after in Champagne. It is a blend of two vintages and two grapes: chardonnay from Avize and still pinot noir from Ambonnay. It has all the Selosse hallmarks of *terroir*, minerality and oxidation but with vinous structure and plump, rather juicy fruit. Although a challenging style, it doesn't need complicated food to enjoy to the full. Just good company and the correct glassware.

Type: Champagne, extra brut, multi-vintage
Style: Galaxy of flavour
Price: £££££
Stockists: Specialist
Toast:
Food: Bresse chicken with morel mushrooms
Occasion: Your own death bed
Website: www.selosse-lesavises.com

Tasting note: *Massively intense, candied fruit, Bakewell tarts, sweet, waxy and floral, smoky and exuberant which follows through to aromas of toasted nuts, seriously funky with some volatile vanilla and orange blossom, oxidative and rich. The palate is gleaming and fleshy, with a mouth-filling viscosity, soft foam and intense freshness. Mineral, razor dry yet exotic and dangerously moreish. Mega!*

27*

JACQUES SELOSSE V.O. GRAND CRU BLANC DE BLANCS

PIONEERS ARE FEW AND FAR BETWEEN IN CHAMPAGNE TODAY, but Anselme Selosse is one. The demand for his tiny annual productions of *terroir*-driven styles means prices of his small range of champagnes are sky-rocketing. He farms the land biodynamically, lowering the yields to get the best flavour concentration and expression per vine. For some traditional champagne drinkers, his wines carry funky flavours as he walks a tightrope of style versus oxidation. I love wines which polarise, and I'm firmly on the favourable side of the fence.

The Version Originale (V.O.) is a multi-vintage blend, based on vintages from three years – 2009, 2008 and 2007 – from three different sites across the Côte des Blancs. The base wine was fermented on old oak barrel, giving flavour and texture to the finished style. This also opens the wines up to oxygen which has a huge effect on flavour and appearance, and you will notice Selosse's champagnes have a richer, golden hue because of it. He uses a solera system for his reserve wines, which adds complexity. Then the wine is aged for up to 42 months in cellar, producing even more rich character, while retaining the mineral backbone from the exceptional Grand Cru chardonnay. Very dry, with less than 1 gram of sugar a bottle, which means you taste every element from the vineyard *terroir*, the unique winemaking and extended cellaring, for a party on your palate.

Type: Champagne, multi-vintage
Style: Daring, limitless enjoyment
Price: £££
Stockists: Specialist
Toast:
Occasion: Checking off a bucket-list dream
Food: Smoked salmon rillettes with cucumber salsa
Website: www.champagnejacquesson.com

Tasting note: *Golden, richer flavours poised with thrilling freshness. The paradoxical style between richness and freshness is thrilling. White peach, brown spice and toasty apple crumble flavours are framed by wild honeyed, ginger on brioche characters, utterly delicious. The mousse is soft and flavoursome, enveloped in a seasoning of funk and mineral poise, leading into a long and complex finish with salty zip.*

28*

JACQUESSON CUVÉE 741

JACQUESSON HAS GONE THROUGH MANY CHANGES SINCE ITS establishment in 1798, but never as radical as when brothers Jean-Hervé and Laurent Chiquet took up the reins in 1988. Challenging their own production every year, further innovations were implemented in 2000 when the entire range of wines was overhauled. Now that the changes have bedded in, Jacquesson is one of the most unique, respected houses in Champagne, reflected in the unusual styles and quality of the wines.

Following the same recipe every year didn't seem right to them and they didn't want to be pigeon-holed into uniformity. The wines they release change each year, and while consistency isn't high on the agenda, quality is foremost. They have flipped the NV model on its head: their NV 700 series is made first, only using their best grapes; all other cuvées come second. Since the brothers began their mission, production has dropped by 40% but they are now one of the most sought-after champagnes, and in the top five producers in the whole region for me.

The name of the cuvée changes every year: it is a production number from their cellar book, which they started with the no. 728 cuvée from the vintage 2000. The Cuvée 741 is based on the 2013 vintage, and their multi-vintage approach shows its true colours, as the 741 shows all the hallmark breadth, depth and complexity that Jacquesson are famous for.

This wine is a blend of 57% chardonnay, 22% pinot meunier and 21% pinot noir, from Jacquesson's holdings across Ay, Dizy, Hautvillers, Avize and Oiry. The wines were entirely vinified in large oak, and held on lees for at least 36 months, and the blend was completed with the addition of special reserve wines. A taste of the extraordinary.

Type: Champagne, extra brut, vintage
Style: Just right Goldilocks
Price: £££££
Stockists: Specialist
Toast:
Food: Turbot on the bone
Occasion: Special anniversary
Website: www.champagnejacquesson.com

Tasting note: *Golden, bone dry and mineral, the first impression of this wine is softly spoken. After some air, the single-vineyard wine gives you an amazing taste of where it's grown. Mineral, chalky and fresh with white peach, almond milk and brioche climaxing in a zippy finish which goes on and on and on.*

29*

JACQUESSON DIZY CORNE BAUTRAY 2007

THE CUVÉE 700 SERIES MAKES UP ALMOST THE ENTIRE PRODUCTION at Jacquesson, so finding the single-vineyard wines can be tricky, but when you do, boy is it worth it. The Cuvée 700 takes priority, so the single-vineyard wines are not made if it will be detrimental to the quality of the 700. Jacquesson only make the single vineyards like the Dizy Corne Bautray when the vintage is just right.

The Corne Bautray is 100% chardonnay from the Dizy vineyard, one of the best chardonnay vineyards in the Vallée de la Marne, an area more recognised for red wine production. This is widely known as one of the greatest wines of the 2007 vintage, a challenging year in the region, and a brilliant expression of this single vineyard. Planted in the 1960s, the Corne Bautray vineyard is steep, south-west facing and rich with alluvial, gravel and chalk soils. 2007 was a cool summer, which heated up towards harvest in September. The 2007 vintage has spent seven and half years on lees, gaining incredible flavours and complexity while remaining electrifyingly fresh. Bottled without dosage means this is a pure taste of the unique *terroir*, and a wine lover's wet dream. It is very rare to taste such an expression of chardonnay, especially from Dizy *terroir*. This vineyard creates grapes which are so delicious that, in 2012, Jean-Hervé found that a wild boar had got into the vineyard and eaten 2,000kg of their chardonnay grapes, over a thousand bottles! If you are lucky enough to find a bottle of this very special wine, make sure the boars don't get to it first.

Type: Champagne, brut, vintage
Style: Priceless white gold
Price: £££££
Stockists: Specialist
Toast:
Food: Salted cashews
Occasion: Selling your first home
Website: www.krug.com

Tasting note: *Foaming white gold, aromas of candied fruits, candle wax and white truffle. It is immediately clear this has intense purity. On the palate, flavours of citrus fruit, vanilla, samurai-like freshness, wild herbs combine pink grapefruit, creamy velvet, tectonic minerality and electrifying finish.*

30*

KRUG CLOS DE MESNIL 2003

JOSEPH KRUG REVOLUTIONISED WHAT CHAMPAGNE CAN BE, REJECTING poor-quality fruit in favour of creating champagnes of great richness and purity. Their production consists only of prestige cuvées, their entry-level champagne is superior to many other houses' top champagnes. Although their infamous multi-vintage the Grande Cuvée (a blend of 120 different base wines) is an icon in Champagne, it is their single-vineyard wines which are the ultimate in rarity and desirability.

The special clos, or walled vineyard, is located in the sleepy town of Le Mesnil-sur-Oger, famous in the Côte des Blancs for the quality of chardonnay grown there, some of the finest in the world. The original vineyard was planted behind a protective wall in the heart of the town in 1698. Krug purchased the vines in 1971; historically the wine was blended into the Grand Cuvée, but the pure class of the 1979 vintage convinced Krug to create a single-vineyard expression. Now, it's probably the most famous vineyard in all of Champagne, a tiny site of just 1.85 hectares planted on east- and south-facing slopes on a bed of pure chalk.

The 2003 vintage was hot across Europe, too hot in places. On paper you wouldn't expect it to be declared a vintage in Champagne, but some of the world's greatest wines always have a degree of magical surprise. There have only been a handful of vintages made since the 1979 vintage: vintages are only made in the years where their stars align, and only ever in tiny quantities. After harvest, the wines are aged in barrel like a fine wine, before spending ten years on lees gaining toast and richness. This champagne is ludicrously expensive, each bottle individually numbered. These wines are collectors' items, one of the greatest champagnes ever made, and will age terrifically well.

Type: Champagne, brut, multi-vintage
Style: Great golden grandeur
Price: ££££
Stockists: High street
Toast: ▢▢▢▢
Food: Hugely versatile – suckling pig, Christmas turkey or eggs benedict with black pudding
Occasion: Your brother's wedding day breakfast
Website: www.krug.com

Tasting note: *Breathtakingly delicious, deep gold in colour, ripe and full of power and flavours of dried apricots, pineapple, marzipan and Christmas cake spices. Mineral freshness keeps the tension of the palate, which is intense and full bodied, caressing you with gingerbread clouds, crème caramel, sugared almonds and buttered brioche waves.*

31*

KRUG GRAND CUVÉE

IT DOESN'T GET MORE SPECIAL THAN KRUG: THE MOST EXPENSIVE, stylish and most luxurious champagne house there is. Krug is the undisputed king of champagne; all hail. And it is a well-known aphrodisiac to boot! But considering the lofty mystique Krug now enjoys, the story started from humble beginnings.

German born Joseph Krug moved to France as a young man and cut his teeth working for Jacquesson Champagne. He was not content with the variable, inconsistent style produced in each vintage, and left at the age of 42 to create a champagne which didn't yet exist: his own Champagne Krug.

The variants in the weather mean that style and quality drastically alter from one year to the next. Joseph's philosophy was craftsmanship without compromise; his goal was to produce the best champagne there had ever been, without the restrictions of vintage variation. He wanted to create a cuvée which was the best expression of champagne, every year without fail. What he achieved revolutionised champagne forever, and the Krug Champagne style is not only evident in bottles of Krug today, but in every house that produces multi-vintage styles.

Krug's non-vintage champagne contains a spread of different vintages, with a higher proportion of older vintage wines in the blend, so the wine style is richer, more flavoursome and complex. Paired with Krug's famous use of oak barrels, this means that Krug's style is one of the richest expressions of champagne there is. Krug houses the most diverse range of reserve wines in the whole of Champagne with access to over 150 wines spanning 10 vintages. With obsessive attention to detail and unfaltering patience, Olivier Krug (Joseph's great-great-grandson) creates wines which are some of the best in the region, and some of the most prestigious. Krug is expensive, it is bottled time, and it's worth it.

Type: Champagne, brut, multi-vintage
Style: Lemon meringue pie
Price: £££
Stockists: High street
Toast:
Food: Sourdough pizza with smoked mozzarella
Occasion: Buying your first flat (if you have any money left)
Website: www.lansonchampagne.com

Tasting note: *Notes of biscuit, shortbread and almonds smash into lemon, spun sugar and ripe apples. Intense and long, with sweet citrus, spice pineapple, samurai freshness and almond croissant notes – this is a champagne of incredible quality and value.*

32*

LANSON EXTRA AGE

ESTABLISHED IN 1760, LANSON IS BASED IN THE HISTORIC CENTRE of Reims, where 9km of cavernous chalk cellars run directly beneath the bustling streets. The same cellars were used during the war as a makeshift village, with a chapel at one end and even a temporary maternity ward at the other. Now it is a more subdued environment, better for the bubbly, where 20 million bottles sit quietly, waiting for their release.

Lanson's hallmark is their crystal-like freshness, achieved by their approach to winemaking, where they keep acidity sharper than many other champagne houses. 'Maintaining freshness, power and fruit' is top of the agenda for new *chef de cave* Hervé Dantan, who is adding his own touch to the classic Lanson style. With Hervé at the helm, the wines will only get better and better.

Lanson is widely distributed, often discounted in supermarkets, and plastered over the TV during Wimbledon, but do not mistake this for a sign of lesser quality. Lanson's Black Label is one of the most sold champagnes in the UK. As Hervé told me, the non-vintage is the most important wine to get right, as these wines sell more than any other. If you are looking for a classic champagne, fresh and fruity, especially on discount, Black Label is serious bang for buck. But for me, it is the top levels of Lanson which get my pulse racing

Created to celebrate 250 years of Lanson, the Extra Age is a combination of Lanson style, vineyard selection and modern chic. Extra Age is created only from Grand Cru vineyards from three separate vintages, with a minimum of ten years on lees. This gives the wine all the time it needs to express the multi-layered complexity of this stunning multi-vintage blend of 60% pinot noir and 40% chardonnay. This is one of the best value prestige cuvées available.

Type: Champagne, brut, vintage
Style: Golden arrow hits the creamy bullseye
Price: £££
Stockists: High street
Toast: 🍞🍞
Food: Salmon on rye, lathered in cream cheese, or hot dogs with that funny American mustard
Occasion: Finishing a crossword
Website: www.lansonchampagne.com

Tasting note: *True to the Lanson house style, this is light, lively and super-classy. A medley of apple charms – granny smith, gala and late-harvest russet – with some depth of caramelised pineapple and nougat. The palate is fresh and super-zingy, with grip and definition giving by the linear saline freshness. There is depth and concentration too, plenty of baked cakes and white stone fruit, showing the quality of Grand Cru vineyards and the stella vintage. Golden, foaming and totally moreish.*

33*

LANSON GOLD LABEL 2008

LANSON CHAMPAGNES ARE AMONG THE MOST READILY AVAILABLE out there, luckily for us as the wines are fresh, moreish and dangerously affordable. Turning heads, and emptying wallets, 2008 was a terrific vintage in champagne and, true to Lanson, the 2008 Gold Label is a prime example of its craftsmanship and the banging vintage.

Lanson's key selling point is its use of non-malolactic fermentation, something which never translates very sexily to the final consumer. What this basically means is the conversion of acids in the wine: malic acids (think Granny Smith apples) to lactic acids (think crème fraîche). When you don't do malolactic, it keeps the wine fresher, leaner and greener. Neither technique is right or wrong, but non-malo styles are rarer, less drinkable in youth but fantastic later. This is the impressive signature of Lanson: the wines do age very, very well.

It wasn't actually until the 1960s that producers started using malolactic fermentation because of improvements in winemaking techniques. With a broad brush, you can say that malo styles of champagne can be drunk quicker, as they do not need as much Lanson ageing, which means customers enjoy the young champagnes, and champagne houses can sell their stock quicker. It's good to have diversity, and hats off to Lanson for championing the 'original' style of champagne.

The 2008 is a blend of Grand Cru vineyards, all vinified separately before the meticulous task of blending the individual components together to create a wine which is more delicious than the sum of its parts. 53% pinot noir gives the blend power and weight, supported by 47% of crystal-like chardonnay which gives minerality, salinity and lubricating refreshment.

Type: Champagne, brut, vintage
Style: Salted caramel surfing
Price: ££££
Stockists: Specialist
Toast: 🍞🍞🍞
Food: Chicken supreme and morel mushrooms
Occasion: Finding long-lost love
Website: www.larmandier.fr

Tasting note: *Golden yellow in colour, the nose is super toasty, very creamy with mango-flesh sweetness. Ripe but agile with some waxy honey, wild savoury notes and an edge of funk. Bliss! On the palate the depth of fruit is remarkable, more mango, pineapple, guava ripe but super chalky; you can taste the vineyard. Then foaming waves of soft, chewy salted caramel and buttered croissants crescendoing in a saline-edged cascade of gushing flavour. Bang tidy.*

34*

LARMANDIER-BERNIER, TERRE DE VERTUS

SINCE 1988 SOPHIE AND PIERRE LARMANDIER HAVE BEEN MAKING spectacular and individual champagne from their vineyards dotted down the spine of the chalk-drenched Côte des Blancs. Pierre can trace his family roots in the region to the French Revolution, and as Sophie says, 'Champagne is in his blood.'
From 1992 they gave up the use of all chemical products and went back to ancient farming methods, leaning towards biodynamic practices which increase the strength and flavour of their finished, natural wines. Their mission: showcasing the unique *terroir* and love affair between chardonnay and chalk in the soils of the Côte des Blancs.

The Terre de Vertus is a single-cru champagne, an expression of this single *terroir* and single vintage, which means the results will change from year to year.

Like the vineyards, the winemaking is minimum intervention; fermentation is with natural yeasts in a mixture of wooden casks and stainless steel tanks. An important factor in the finished style is that the finished base wine is left on the natural lees for a year with gentle stirring. This technique is common in Burgundy where the world's best still chardonnay is made as the method gives complexity, richness and funky aromas. The wines are unfiltered when they go into secondary fermentation and left on lees in the cellars for at least four years, then are bottled without any addition of sugar. The results are unique and pure, more 'vinous' or wine-like than many in the region, and you fully feel the authenticity of the vineyards and quality of fruit. Their wines are beautiful on release, but will age incredibly well if you can resist.

Type: Champagne rosé, brut, vintage
Style: Burgundian brilliance meets champagne magic
Price: £££££
Stockists: High Street
Toast: 🍞🍞🍞
Food: Pigeon breast with cranberries
Occasion: Your first godchild's christening
Website: www.laurent-perrier.com

Tasting note: *Red fruit, satin, velvet with a touch of dusty stately home in a polished and comfy sort of way. Layered and complex like few other rosés. Warm spices of cinnamon and nutmeg, Maraschino cherry and mineral flashes. Vinous, with bags of Burgundian character; gamey, savoury, and sweetmeat notes. Foaming, cloud-like purity like a foaming Grand Cru burgundy, elegance and complexity rarely found in champagne rosé. Layers of savoury fruit, rosés, earthy, savoury sweetness and dry, bracing cherry acid, chalk finish, mineral and saline in length.*

35*

LAURENT-PERRIER CUVÉE ALEXANDRA 2004

LAURENT PERRIER WAS THE FIRST HOUSE TO LAUNCH ROSÉ EN MASSE AND their iconic Rosé Brut is the best selling champagne rosé in the world. It was a natural step for Laurent-Perrier to use their skills to craft a prestige cuvée rosé. Head-honcho Bernard de Nonancourt created Cuvée Alexandra as his top expression of vintage rosé for the wedding of his daughter Alexandra in 1987. If you like champagne rosé, it doesn't get much better than this. But it isn't for everyone. The Cuvée Rosé multi-vintage for LP is juicy, fruity and has mass appeal, the Alexandra on the other hand is delicate, *terroir* driven and subtle, so would be better appreciated in a relaxed setting, rather than an al-fresco garden party.

The 2004 Alexandra rosé is only the seventh release since its launch over 30 years ago. Made from 80% pinot noir from some of the best Grand Cru vineyards in the region in Ambonnay and Bouzy, the wines have amazing pinot character of fruit and expression. 20% is chardonnay, also from Grand Cru sites in Avize, Cramant and Le Mesnil-sur-Oger which gives this wine incredible freshness and longevity.

The delicate pink salmon colour was obtained by the bleeding method, where both the chardonnay and pinot noir grapes are macerated for three days to soak up colour, flavour and wine-like characters. The cellaring is long for the Alexandra, a minimum of 10 years before release. But youth is on her side, and although the wine is approaching 15 years of age, it still sparkles with youthful *joie de vivre*.

Type: Champagne rosé, brut, multi-vintage
Style: Rose petal bath bomb
Price: £££
Stockists: High street
Toast:
Food: Seared tuna steaks with lime and chilli, steak tartare or homemade raspberry tartlets
Occasion: Candlelit romantic night in
Website: www.laurent-perrier.com

Tasting note: A glass of pink exuberance: cherry, strawberry, red fruit, those bootlace sweeties fill your taste buds, a richly textured palate thick with strawberries and clotted cream with a wash of cleansing chalky freshness. The finish is round and spicy, uplifted with rosewater with a turn of cracked black pepper.

36*

LAURENT-PERRIER CUVÉE ROSÉ

When you arrive at LP, the initial impact is its stately size and the beautifully manicured French gardens, as you would expect from the fourth largest champagne producer. Nestled in front of the grand facade of Maison Laurent Perrier is a statue of a young boy peeing into a pond, with the words '*Ne Buvez Jamais d'Eau*' transcribed beside him. This is LP: serious, sizable, impeccably turned out but also good fun. Laurent Perrier's varied and fascinating story stretches back two hundred years, but it was the legendary Bernard de Nonancourt who was the tour de force behind LP's post-war success. He changed the fate of this family champagne house after fighting courageously in the French Army and then the Resistance. He lost his dear brother Maurice, who would have been at the helm of the company if he had survived the war, to Nazi barbarism.

Before 1968, when LP launched their rosé, pink champagne wasn't a popular style. Although rosé champagne was invented a long time before this, it was LP that broke the mould with this pink fizzy dreamboat, a revolutionary multi-vintage rosé, and thus a whole category was born. To this day the Cuvée Rosé is an icon in its field, a benchmark of quality and one of the most sought-after and drunk rosé fizzers. Brand equity aside, it is bloody delicious.

This is 100% pinot noir sourced from a multitude of cru vineyards, many Grand Cru from Montaigne de Reims, including Bouzy, famous for its exceptional pinot noir. It is macerated like a red wine for two to three days to draw out colour, flavour and texture from the grape skins, which gives LP rosé a rich style with bags of fruit, wine-like character, volume on the palate and champagne magic. A minimum of five years in cellars at Tours-sur-Marne before release is manifest in this pink delight.

Type: Champagne, brut zero, vintage
Style: Kissing a margarita on a stormy sea
Price: £££££
Stockists: Very specialist
Toast: 🍞🍞🍞
Food: Salt-baked bass with beurre blanc and sorrel
Occasion: Your birthday present, from yourself
Website: http://leclercbriant.fr/uk

Tasting note: *Edgy fruit of fresh-cut lemons and limes, wild honey, oxidative character, wild and funky, complex and saline, like the lip-puckering taste of the first sip of a salt-rimmed margarita. The fruit is white peach and green-apple crumble, vanilla custard mixed with iodine, floral perfume and an extraordinary balance of sour and sweet fruit which tantalises the taste buds and has you gasping for another saline hit. There is sweet spice of oak which frames this pure and racing champagne. Long, moving and complex. WOW.*

37*

LECLERC BRIANT ABYSS BRUT ZERO 2012

Leclerc Briant has established itself as a hyper-trendy, quality producer creating modern but respectful wines. Founded in 1872, the house has gone through numerous changes. Now under the watchful eye of Frédéric Zeimett and sixth-generation *vigneron* Ségolène Leclerc, they obtained organic and biodynamic certification for the entire estate, with two goals: to respect mother nature and to bring out the true character of the *terroir* in their wines. With singular focus in both vineyards and winery, they use biodynamic principles (often a buzz word rather than a quality reference – not true for Leclerc Briant). The wines carry a character I call 'funk', a wild savoury note, like many world-class wines, due to their wild fermentation and natural, oxidative winemaking.

I've tasted a lot of wine, and, luckily for me, a lot of champagne. I rarely get really surprised by wine these days; it's harder to find the unique gems when you've been round the block. But the cuvée Abyss blew my mind. Based on the 2012 vintage, it is a blend of chardonnay, pinot noir and meunier, all vinified and aged in oak barrels from wines specifically selected from vineyards with ancient marine limestone soils.

The bottles are then aged for two years in their house cellars as usual. Corked without additional sugar (brut zero) so the resulting style is razor dry. Now, hold your breath. Then the bottles are aged off the coast of Brittany on the sea bed at a depth of 60 metres. Fifteen months later, the bottles emerge covered in maritime micro-organisms including mussels, barnacles and seaweed, which give an amazing tactile finish to this unique bottle of fizz. Is this is an expensive gimmick? Yes, but its impact on flavour is what's exciting. The results are mind-boggling.

Type: Champagne, brut nature, vintage
Style: Gentle sunny freshness
Price: ££££
Stockists: High street
Toast: 🍞🍞
Food: pickled veg, pitta and baba ganoush
Occasion: Sunday night, on a bank holiday
Website: www.louis-roederer.com

Tasting note: *Clean, modern fruit, open and immediate with ripe yellow plums, spice and sunshine citrus. Fresh and pure: white flowers, peach skin and hazelnuts mingle and charm one another in an abstract chaos. Ending in a razor-sharp purity and fine, elegant bubbles, so typical of the Roederer style.*

38*

LOUIS ROEDERER CHAMPAGNE BRUT NATURE 2009

BECAUSE OF CAREFUL FARMING, THE ROEDERER HARVESTS ARE OFTEN 30% lower than its neighbours, but the increased class of each grape makes up for the smaller volume. The attention to detail is immense; and for highly respected *chef de cave* Jean-Baptiste his objective is to let his wines express the wonderful *terroirs*. He explained to me that in blending there is a universal rule: if you add a weak wine to 10 good wines, you make a bad wine. Only good wines make up Roederer blends. He describes himself as a conductor, blending the right music to create the Roederer universe, and wants as much diversity as possible when creating his blends.

The Brut Nature is a collaboration between Roederer CEO Frédéric Rouzaud and French designer Philippe Starck, who encouraged Roederer to be innovative in the quest for the perfect champagne. This could be said to be contrary to the general Roederer philosophy of letting the vineyards express themselves, but the results are popular and thirst-quenching.

The grapes are grown on Coteaux de Cumières on cool, clay-based soils, contrary to Roederer's affection for chalk, giving a different profile to the finished champagne. Brut Nature wines, which only permit 2.25g of sugar per bottle, have become more popular, particularly when they are as good as this one. It is a blend of pinot noir, meunier and chardonnay, all harvested and pressed on the same day. A quarter of the blend was vinified in oak barrels, imparting an oak spice to the finish, and five years resting in the cellars give it unworldly deliciousness . . . This is the cutting edge of cool and tastes like a laser beam.

Type: Champagne, brut, vintage
Style: Top of the Pops
Price: £££££
Stockists: High street
Toast: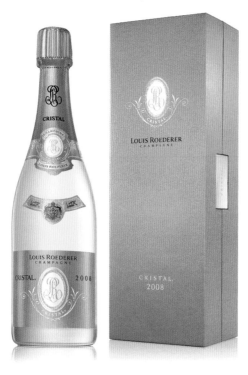
Food: Victoria Sponge
Occasion: Granny's 90th birthday
Website: www.louis-roederer.com

Tasting note: *It doesn't get better than this, an expression of the best vineyards in all of champagne. Precious, harmonious and fresh, this wine ripples with energy and tantalises with flavours of lemon meringue, chalky salinity, candied fruits, salted caramel bonbons, green apples caked in toffee glaze and crunchy honeycomb; the foam is endless and seamless and the finish is so moreish, it should be illegal.*

39*

LOUIS ROEDERER CRISTAL 2008

FOUNDED IN 1776 AND STILL UNDER FAMILY OWNERSHIP, LOUIS Roederer is perhaps most famous for its prestige cuvée Cristal. At Roederer they make fine wine first and bubbles second, but for the *chef de cave*, legendary Jean-Baptiste Lecaillon, expressing the sense of place is paramount. Roederer is one of the largest producers of biodynamic and organic vineyards in Europe. 'Chalk is the style of Roederer, and Cristal is a celebration of chalk.'

Their single-estate Cristal has long been a favourite of the rich and famous. The Russian royal family enjoyed Roederer's wines so much that in 1876 Tsar Alexander II asked Roederer to reserve the best cuvée for him, and thus Cristal was born. Alexander II was so paranoid about being assassinated he wanted a clear glass to be able to check that nothing untoward had been slipped inside, as bottles are historically dark, green glass.

The Cristal 2008 is the first ever vintage to undergo a full ten years of ageing before release, and the first time Louis Roederer has released Cristal vintages non-consecutively after Cristal 2009 launched in 2017. There has been a huge amount of hype regarding the 2008, a near perfect vintage. Many critics around the world believe this is the best Cristal ever made. When asked to comment, *chef de cave* Lecaillon said '2008 is almost my dream', so there must be a little room for improvement!

The wine is 60% pinot noir, 40% chardonnay. A touch of oak builds further complexity, but it is all about the vineyards in Cristal; it's as chalky as a blackboard. The 2008 offers amazing generosity on release, unlike some other recent Cristal vintages, which means it is drinking beautifully now. Jean-Baptiste says 'Champagne is time in a bottle. And the true luxury of champagne is time.' I agree, but if I had a bottle of Cristal in my cellar, it wouldn't last long before I popped the cork and drank like a Tsar.

Type: Champagne, brut, multi-vintage
Style: Starry-eyed pop pleaser
Price: ££
Stockists: Everywhere
Toast: 🍞🍞
Food: Late night chicken shawarma
Occasion: When fizz is the only option
Website: www.moet.com

Tasting note: *Tastes a lot like champagne: slightly sweet, fruity, very fizzy and refreshing.*

40*

MOËT & CHANDON
BRUT IMPÉRIAL

FIRST OFF: YOU PRONOUNCE THE 'T' IN MOËT – IT IS ORIGINALLY a Dutch name. The house is integral to the development and success of champagne, and the region, wine and company have grown up and developed together since Claude Moët established Maison Moët et Cie in 1743.

Claude had an influence establishing champagne as the drink of choice for nobility through his connections in the royal courts of Versailles. When the masses knew their royal family was enjoying wine from Champagne, everyone wanted a taste of the high life. It was Claude's grandson Jean-Rémy who took the company to the lofty heights of success. He toured the world selling the champagne lifestyle to royalty, and had a close friendship with Napoleon Bonaparte. Jean-Rémy maximised this celebrity endorsement as powerful marketing leverage, and orders began pouring in so fast he could barely keep up with demand, the springboard of success that the company still enjoys today.

Moët dedicated their bestselling champagne in Napoleon's honour in 1869; this dedication can still be seen today on every bottle of Brut Impérial. Moët & Chandon is still the world's most drunk champagne, representing almost 10% of the region's total production. People love to hate large corporate conglomerates, but the quality is remarkably sound considering the enormity of the operation.

A blend of over 100 different wines from LVMH's massive 6,000 hectares of vineyards, this wine is a straight 40% pinot noir, 40% pinot meunier and 20% chardonnay, balanced by 30% of reserve wines for consistency. This is often people's first taste of champagne, and it is the quality benchmark of the entire region.

Type: Champagne, brut, vintage
Style: Peaches and cream
Price: ££££
Stockists: High street
Toast: 🍞🍞
Food: Tartiflette or cheesy biscuits
Occasion: Aprés ski, or post sledging
Website: www.perrier-jouet.com

Tasting note: *Tinned peaches, cream and honeysuckle jump from the glass. Fresh and oozingly enjoyable with a wash of citrus freshness propelled by burnt shortbread character and a mouthful of summer fruits and mineral zappiness.*

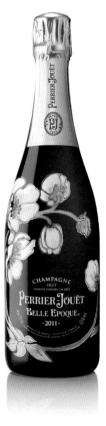

41*

PERRIER-JOUËT BELLE ÉPOQUE 2011

FOUNDED IN 1811 WHEN PIERRE-NICHOLAS PERRIER MARRIED YOUNG beauty Adèle Jouët, Pierrier Jouët set up shop on the Avenue de Champagne, Épernay.

La Belle Époque (Beautiful Era) was a golden time in European history, between the end of the Franco-Prussian War in 1871 and the outbreak of the First World War in 1914. It was a time of peace, economic prosperity, and technological and cultural revolution. Paris became THE place to be, the Moulin Rouge was in full swing, and the bars of Paris were flowing and swaying with absinthe and champagne. Post-impressionists like Picasso, Matisse, Gauguin were painting, boozing and schmoozing at the time, and it was for this defining moment in high culture that the top cuvée from PJ is named. Art Nouveau was born, still celebrated today in the Paris metro station signs, and on every bottle of Belle Époque.

The Japanese anemones engraved into every bottle of Belle Époque are testament to the Modernist movement celebrating the dawn of the twentieth century. The emerging middle classes had more money to spend on luxury goods, fine foods, with one increasingly popular drink which encapsulated the time of prosperity: champagne.

The 2011 prestige cuvée celebrates the 200th anniversary of Perrier-Jouet. *Chef de cave* Hervé Deschamps has combined 50% chardonnay from Grand Cru Cramant and Avize, 45% pinot noir from Montagne de Reims with a cheeky splash of 5% pinot meunier from Dizy, a recipe for success. Over six years cellaring in the PJ cellars mean that this bottle is raucously delicious now. Pour yourself a coupe and take yourself to the grand boulevards of gay Paris.

Type: Champagne, vintage, brut
Style: Fizzy white burgundy
Price: £££££
Stockists: Specialist
Toast: 🍞🍞🍞🍞🍞
Food: Chicken korma
Occasion: World Peace
Website: www.philipponnat.com

Tasting note: *Golden in colour, frothy and elegant. The neb is full, pineapple, McIntosh-Red apple, vanilla custard, smoke and bouquet-garnier herbs, inviting and open. The palate is full, rich and burgundian paired with mineral zippy freshness. The flavours weave together with spiced apple, firework smoke, gingerbread and artisan perry. It's burgundy with bubbles. Absolutely bloody brilliant.*

42*

PHILIPPONNAT CLOS DES GOISSES 2007

THE PHILIPPONNAT FAMILY HAVE CULTIVATED VINES IN AY SINCE 1552 and have been making decent plonk for almost half a millennium. Based in the Vallée de la Marne, on the pivotal edge of all three regions of Champagne, they are privileged to have the oldest, and one of the greatest, clos vineyards of the whole region. Clos des Goisses is soaked in legend and myth, and makes some of the most powerful and rich-tasting wines in all Champagne. Geographically and climatically special, this special walled vineyard lies on the east of Mareuil-sur-Ay at the very heart of the region where the Côte des Blancs, Vallée de la Marne and Montagne de Reims meet.

Gois means very steep slope in the local dialect: the vineyard is positively alpine at 45° making it very difficult to work and harvest each year. It faces directly south towards the river Marne which reflects the sun with even more intensity towards these special, ancient vines. This is one of the warmest places in Champagne, with temperatures parallel to Burgundy in the south, and shielding walls protecting the vines from the winds. The soil is pure chalk, and the old vines soak up all the minerality and personality of this special plot.

A blend of 65% pinot noir and 35% chardonnay, with partial vinification in oak barrels, gives complexity and white Burgundian wine-like character. There is no malolactic fermentation; the fruit character is ripe and juicy balanced by retained steely acidity and *terroir* character. Extended ageing on lees for over ten years in the historic Philipponnat cellars gives the wine remarkable toasted weight, smoky freshness and spicy aromatics. The dose is kept low, at around 3 grams of sugar per bottle, to showcase the pure expression of this exceptional vineyard.

Type: Champagne rosé, brut, multi-vintage
Style: Pink lightning
Price: £££
Stockists: Specialist
Toast:
Food: Line-caught trout with horseradish cream
Occasion: Not participating in dry-January
Website: www.champagne-peters.com

Tasting note: *Redcurrants, pink peppercorns and grapefruit play a euphoric dance on your palate. The nose is packed with red fruits, your senses caressed with a rose and floral perfume. The palate is fuller than expected, dense fruit from the pinot meunier with a blissful spike of Côte des Blancs minerality. Fine bubbles and great length, altogether a touch of magic.*

43*

PIERRE PÉTERS ROSÉ FOR ALBANE

CHAMPAGNE GROWER–PRODUCER PIERRE PÉTERS IS KNOWN TO BE ONE of the most dedicated *terroir* producers in Champagne. Based in the heart of the Côte des Blancs in the village of Le Mesnil-sur-Oger, the family have been making mind-boggling fizz for six generations. They have specialised in Grand Cru blanc de blancs champagnes since 1919, and their grapes come exclusively from their own vineyards in Le Mesnil-sur-Oger and nearby Oger, Avize and Cramant.

Vine maturity matters; Pierre Péters' vines have an average age of 30 years. They produce grapes that are flavourful and mineral, as the roots have had three decades to dig deep into the tight, white chalk bedrock to soak up precious flavours and minerals. As with many of the best producers in Champagne, *terroir* is fundamental, and the Pierre Péters range is driven by expression of their sense of place. Their single-vineyard champagne, Les Chétillons, is rarer than a mystic unicorn and one of world's best champagnes.

The house is now run by the talented Rodolphe Péters, and this rosé is the wildcard in their range. Created for Rodolphe's daughter Albane in 2007, it is their only wine not to be 100% sourced from their own vines in the Côte des Blancs. Instead it is a blend of their own mineral-flecked chardonnay from Le Mesnil-sur-Oger and a red pinot meunier sourced from Damery and Cumières in Vallée de la Marne. The result is an electric rosé, with mass appeal, bags of crunchy red fruit and spades of pure chalky minerality which will tickle, please and delight novice and the most expert palates.

Type: Champagne, brut, vintage
Style: Inspiringly salivating
Price: £££££
Stockists: Specialist
Toast:
Food: Pot roast pheasant or cheese fondue
Occasion: Winning at life
Website: www.polroger.co.uk

Tasting note: *Intense and complex, this is an incredible champagne of seriousness and total drinkability. Dried fruits, toasted almonds and honey with yogurt fill your glass and wine senses. There is such skill in the way the fizz cuts through the full-bodied and powerfully flavoured palate. You are left gasping for more, with burnt butter, ripe pear and tarte tatin flavours framed by remarkable freshness and a salty citrus edge.*

'A single glass of champagne impacts a feeling of exhilaration. The nerves are braced, the imagination is agreeably stirred, the wits become more nimble. A bottle produces the opposite effect.'
WINSTON CHURCHILL

44*

POL ROGER CUVÉE SIR WINSTON CHURCHILL 2006

POL ROGER NAMED THEIR TOP CUVÉE AFTER THEIR MOST FAMOUS customer: Churchill was such a devoted champagne fan that it was said that he preferred to have his own bottle beside him on the dinner table 'to be independent of the vagaries of butlers'.

During the Second World War the production and buying of champagne was controlled by the Wehrmacht. The orders for the Führer provided the Resistance and British Forces with important military intelligence: the vast shipments enabled them to pre-empt where the Germans were sending their armies to attack next.

Because of the demands of the thirsty Nazis, many champagne houses revolted and sent fake products in place of their usual high quality. Some got away with this, but those who were caught were imprisoned or worse. Many champagne houses were threatened with closure as they were literally being drunk dry. Pol Roger ran this risk. In 1941, the Comité Interprofessionnel du Vin de Champagne (CIVC) was established to protect the Champenois on a united front. The CIVC helped Pol Roger when they needed 'urgent repairs' to their winery to meet the German needs. When they were supplied with materials, Pol Roger used the cement to wall up and hide their top champagnes!

Although the blend is a closely guarded secret, we know it is only made in the best years, and is a dual blend of pinot noir and chardonnay, sourced from Grand Cru vineyards which were already producing grapes in Churchill's lifetime. These older vines give rich and complex wines, further benefited by extended cellaring. As the great man said, 'My tastes are simple. I am easily satisfied with the best.' With the Cuvée Winston, this is exactly what you're getting.

Type: Champagne, brut, multi-vintage
Style: Silky superiority
Price: £££
Stockists: High street
Toast: 🍞🍞
Food: Posh fish and chips (i.e. with a knife and fork)
Occasion: Successfully building something from Ikea
Website: www.polroger.co.uk

Tasting note: *Golden straw in colour, the bubbles are fine and attractive. Flavours of pear, mango and white flowers fill the aromas and the palate is bursting with notes of ripe citrus, golden apples, honey vanilla brioche, quince and zesty tangerine. Long-lasting and layered in flavour, delicious.*

45*

POL ROGER 'WHITE FOIL' BRUT RÉSERVE

ESTABLISHED IN 1849, NOW IN THE FIFTH GENERATION OF FAMILY ownership, Pol keeps true to its principles of unfaltering quality and integrity of style. Few champagnes are as British as Pol Roger; you will notice the British coat of arms on each bottle. This royal warrant means Pol Roger has been the purveyor of champagne to the Queen and the British royal family since 1877. Pol is the Queen's favourite champagne, and the iconic White Foil Brut Réserve was the fizz poured at Kate and Will's wedding. Over the years, Pol has carved a reputation as one of the leading, most respected of all champagnes houses.

The winery is located just off the Avenue du Champagne. Travelling down this street is like walking down Champagne's Hall of Fame, with each house more famous than the last. But the home of Pol Roger is up a little side street tucked away from the immediate hustle and bustle, the address: 1 Rue Winston Churchill. The grand house of Pol Roger, which until recently was the family home, sits on top of the polished and clinical winery below. Open the door in the back of the fermentation hall and you are led down to dark and humid chalk cellars, the deepest in Épernay, reaching 33 metres underground in a network of caves and tunnels where 8 million bottles of Pol rest quietly before release.

Pol Roger's flagship wine 'White Foil' Brut Réserve is a blend of equal parts of chardonnay, pinot noir and pinot meunier sourced from 30 different vineyards all over Champagne, including Grand Cru sites in the Côte des Blancs. It is aged for four years in Pol's cellars, adding richness and complexity before release.

Type: Champagne, brut, multi-vintage
Style: Juicy pears and bags of flair
Price: ££
Stockists: High street
Toast: 🍞🍞
Food: Eggs benny
Occasion: Breakfast of champions
Website: www.ruinart.com

Tasting note: *Light and fruity with bags of apple, ripe pear and Starburst lemon and lime. Subtle spices of cayenne and white pepper season the palate with honeysuckle and flashes of grapefruit. Super-fresh, super-clean, fruity and super-delicious.*

46*

RUINART BLANC DE BLANCS

RUINART IS THE WORLD'S OLDEST CHAMPAGNE HOUSE, FOUNDED by Dom Ruinart's nephew Nicolas in 1729. This was one year after Louis XV allowed champagne houses to sell their wine in bottles, opening up export trade and changing champagne forever. Young Nicolas was an ambitious and talented man, full of beans and charm. Sparkling wine was a brand new product at the time young Nicolas was flogging it around Europe, Russia and latterly the USA. Champagne houses have some of the strongest brand equity of any product on the planet, and you need great communication skills and a strong story to persuade customers to spend £30+ on a bottle. Champagne's branding and marketing nowadays, although often over the top, is the legacy of these few intrepid salesmen who first started to market their wines directly to consumers.

Ruinart is now part of the luxury goods conglomerate LVMH, the humble one on the team sheet behind Moët, Veuve and Krug – but by no means is it lesser. Chardonnay is king for Ruinart, and their blanc de blancs styles are the benchmark of champagne, portrayed in their eighteenth-century bell-shaped bottle, which is a nod to their long history. The man at the helm is now smooth-talking Frédéric Panaiotis, a self-acclaimed fiend for chardonnay. What I also like about Ruinart is that they are one of the few major champagne houses that produce more for the French market than they export, a good gauge of quality, as the French have been drinking it for almost 300 years.

A blend of many different chardonnay components from Montagne de Reims and Côte des Blancs, this is one of the benchmark styles of blanc de blancs. A blend of three different vintages, and 25% reserve wines, this champagne will develop round and nutty flavours if you are patient enough to age it.

Type: Champagne, brut, blanc de blancs, vintage
Style: Just wait; you will be rewarded
Price: £££££
Stockists: Very specialist
Toast:
Food: Your desert island dish!
Occasion: Your 100th birthday
Website: www.salondelamotte.com

Tasting note: *The aromas are lifted and layered with white flowers, ginger, honeysuckle and toasted hazelnuts. The palate is a tightrope walk of chalk, backed by orange and candied citrus, freshly buttered croissants and sea spray salinity: sensual chaos. Over the years this champagne will transform into a spectacular celebration of chardonnay, gaining richness in texture and weight, showcasing one of the greatest vineyards on the planet, and the longevity and quality of wines which hail from it.*

47*

SALON BLANC DE BLANCS 2004

LE MESNIL IS BUILT ON A BEDROCK OF PURE CHALK WHICH RISES TO the surface on the slope towards the top of the Côte des Blancs. The vineyards here are recognised as being some of the finest chardonnay vineyards in the world, for the vines' rampant love affair with chalk. Champagne growers can charge an extra premium for the wine here, not only because of the quality of the wines, but also due to the reputation of one estate whose champagnes are some of the most sought after and expensive in the world. This is Champagne Salon.

Founder Eugène-Aimé Salon pioneered Champagne's first ever blanc de blancs in the early 1900s. The famous branded 'S' on Salon bottles represents a single wine, a single grape, a single vineyard, a single time and one man's singular vision. He was a driven man with one mission: to find the holy coupe. This wine was originally destined only for personal consumption; the first commercial vintage was in 1921. Nowadays the mystique is slightly diluted, but by no means less special, as Laurent Perrier own and produce both Salon and brother Delamotte Champagne. For champagne connoisseurs, Salon is the world's most sought-after champagne and the quintessential blanc de blancs. The wine is only produced in the best years, on average only three each decade. These wines need time to open, develop and evolve: the Maison suggest a drinking window to start of 20–30 years. If you do find a bottle, which is difficult and expensive, do put it away for another few years, and when you get round to opening it, pray it isn't corked!

Type: Champagne, blanc de blancs, vintage
Style: A crisp caress
Price: ££££
Stockists: High street
Toast:
Food: Poached chicken breast, crispy salted skin and pickled mushrooms
Occasion: Brother's graduation dinner
Website: www.taittinger.com

Tasting note: *Bright lemon and candy apples dance with white flowers and honey on the nose. The palate is a wash of sunshine peachy fruit and Williams pears pricked with cloves. The taste of the lemon curd on oatcakes and the sublime* terroir *manifests with the sensation of chalk, sea shells and smoke, which draws out this long and elegant wine.*

48 *

TAITTINGER COMTES DE CHAMPAGNE 2006

TAITTINGER IS ONE OF THE OLDEST AND MOST FAMOUS CHAMPAGNE houses, founded in 1734, and is a considerable force as the region's sixth largest producer. For its size and wide distribution, the quality stacks, and the company is very consistent across its large range of champagnes.

The Taittinger logo recalls the emblem of Hugo the First, the Comte de Champagne who ruled the region in the eleventh century and was one of the Knights Templar, founders of the Champagne region. The company is now part of a larger commercial enterprise, but still partially owned by the original Taittinger family, President Pierre-Emmanuel Taittinger, son Clovis and daughter Vitalie. Taittinger is the first champagne producer to invest in vines in the south of England, buying a majority share of Domaine Evremond in Kent, but we will have to wait until 2023 for our first taste.

The flagship Comtes de Champagne is a different story altogether, and a serious step above any other in the range. It is one of the most consistent and desirable of all champagnes, a favourite of mine from my *sommelier* days. First produced in 1952 and only produced in the top years, this is a true benchmark of a blanc de blancs. 2006 was a hot year which translated into an open and fruity style. Only sourced from prime-time vineyards in the Côte des Blancs, including Avize and Le Mesnil-sur-Oger, this wine showcases the hallmark minerality of the chalky soils. Aged in the Taittinger cellars in Reims for up to 10 years before release, this chardonnay evolves richness and amazing toastiness accentuated by a proportion of the blend which is aged in oak barrel. This is drinking like a boss now, but will continue to develop for 10 to 20 years.

Type: Champagne, brut, blanc de noirs, vintage
Style: Christmas cake came early
Price: ££££
Stockists: Specialist
Toast: 🍞🍞🍞🍞
Food: Chana masala
Occasion: Quit your job, left your partner and you're running away to the circus
Website: www.tarlant.com

Tasting note: *Yellow plums stuffed with ginger and wild honey, succulent on the palate with golden, foaming, creamy richness. The extended time on lees gives rich toasty, spicy, sweet flavours, like a Christmas cake smoothie. Freshness, fruit, roasted nuts and super moreish. The finish is all butterscotch foam, chalk and a touch of a good Sex on the Beach.*

49 *

TARLANT LA VIGNE D'OR BLANC DE MEUNIERS 2004

TARLANT IS ONE OF THE GREAT PRODUCERS OF VALLÉE DE LA Marne, based in the town of Oeuilly. The family can trace back their winemaking rootstock to 1648. The property is still a family affair, each member fiercely proud of their vineyards and how to best express them in the bottle. Benoît Tarlant now runs the estate and has made his own changes since coming on board in 1999. The sugar was the first thing to go; most of the Tarlant champagnes have no added sugar, they are pure expressions of the diverse vineyard and the skill of the winemaker.

The fermentation for Benoît's wines is generally done in barrel, some steel tanks and some clay amphora. There are no set rules here; it totally depends on the grapes of the vintage. La Vigne d'Or (The Golden Vine) is a single-vineyard champagne from vines over 50 years old. The soil here is a particular mix of clay and chalk unique to the Marne Valley. This *terroir* allows the pinot meunier vines to really express themselves, both mineral from the chalk and richly fruity from the clay.

It is unusual to have a 100% pinot meunier champagne, especially of such incredible quality. Most producers blend it away into wider homogenous blends only to be lost behind the more structured chardonnay or pinot noir grapes.

After harvesting in September 2004, the vinification took place in oak over four weeks, with lees stirring, which adds creamy flavours and more body to the wine. The still wine is kept in barrel, like a fine burgundy, until May, gaining complexity and wild, spicy flavours. Put in bottle, and 11 years later, this razor-dry champagne is truly memorable. La Vigne d'Or proves that Tarlant produce some of the best in town, and that pinot meunier is capable of great wines.

Type: Champagne, brut, non-vintage
Style: Fruity, toasty, tasty
Price: ££
Stockists: Everywhere
Toast: 🍞🍞🍞
Food: Party blinis and parmesan croquettes
Occasion: You don't need one!
Website: www.veuveclicquot.com

Tasting note: *Oozing richness, character and fullness of fruit in the gushing forward style of the house. Golden yellow with white fruits, raisins, vanilla and brioche. Fruity and toasty, with a hint of spice.*

50*

VEUVE CLICQUOT BRUT YELLOW LABEL

Barbe-Nicole Clicquot, née Ponsardin, was born in Reims at the time of the French revolution. Widowed before the age of 30, she renamed the small business she shared with her late husband as Veuve (Widow) Clicquot and without experience she transformed her tiny family enterprise into one of the greatest champagne businesses in history. The great ladies of Champagne have done much to empower women in business, and none more so than Barbe-Nicole. A skilled innovator, she had a profound and lasting influence on the marketing, selling and production of champagne. Not happy with the champagne quality of her time, she pioneered two vital production methods – disgorgement and riddling – changing the wine from murky, cloudy wine to the bright clear wine we know today.

Today owned by LVMH, Veuve is one of the most famous champagnes. The label was originally white and the wine a sweeter style; the now iconic 'Yellow Label' was invented for the UK market in 1877, catering for our drier palates. The use of large vats is now an important feature for Veuve; the base wine has one year in wood giving the style subtle spice and full texture in the mouth. The wine is a blend from 60 different vineyards from all over Champagne, with a dominance of pinot noir. A third of the blend is from Veuve's special reserves wines, dating back 30 years, which add complexity and roundness. To this day, Veuve remains one of the greatest champagne brands, a direct salute to Madame Clicquot. Apart from Dom Pérignon, there has been no one so influential as Veuve Clicquot, and we champagne drinkers have much to thank her for. Next time you pop a bottle of Veuve, make sure you raise it to the young, pioneering widow who changed champagne forever.

Type: Champagne, brut, vintage
Style: Getting spanked by a velvet cushion
Price: ££££
Stockists: Specialist
Toast: 🍞🍞🍞
Food: Fuller fish dishes: shellfish, monkfish, John Dory; or langoustines with lemongrass
Occasion: Forgetting 2016 ever happened
Website: www.veuveclicquot.com

Tasting note: *Sparkling gold. Full bodied, a generous style with bags of flavour. White cherries, red apple compote on shortbread, with a mineral, chalky back palate. Long, persistent finish which just makes you wanna drink more of it!*

51*

VEUVE CLICQUOT LA GRANDE DAME 2006

1811 WAS A POIGNANT YEAR FOR THE CHAMPAGNE REGION – THE sky was illuminated by the flight of a starlit comet which many took to be a good luck charm. As it transpired, the quality of the harvest was the best on record. At this time champagne bottles weren't labelled or branded in any way. At Veuve, Madame Clicquot started to brand each cork with a comet star symbol to mark the special vintage and distinguish her champagnes from others. And so the first ever champagne brand was born. You will see comet star symbols still used on many champagnes (and in this book!) paying homage to the famous 1811 vintage.

Named after the great woman of champagne, La Grande Dame is Veuve's flagship wine. Only using grapes from vineyards Madame Clicquot would have known or bought herself, it is blended from eight Grands Crus across the region, including Bouzy, Ambonnay and Oger. I've got a lot of time for all Veuve Clicquot wines; the quality stacks considering the enormity of production. But for La Grande Dame, annual production is small, and it is only made in the best years. Marketing budgets aside, you really do get what you pay for here: the quality is outstanding.

2006 was a turbulent year in Champagne: a hot summer and variable August meant grapes had to be hand sorted to find the best of the bunch. La Grande Dame, in Veuve style, is a pinot-dominant blend which gives the wine roundness and fruit intensity, while the rest of the blend is chardonnay, giving balancing freshness, elegance and direction. This is an exceptional champagne, worthy of cellaring. The house recommends drinking this up to 2025. Although this wine will age terrifically well, if I had a bottle I'd open it this evening.

THE SPARKLERS

★

Understanding sparklers

★

Champagne is the frontman in the sparkling tune, but there is a gospel choir of backing singers, and it is often where the undiscovered talent hides. Champagne's acceptance is ingrained in us because of its longevity as well as its quality. But the world of sparkling wine is changing. Developments in technology are one factor, but so too is the change in climate and our own tastes.

The following 50 fizzers are benchmark examples of why you don't always need champagne. Many of my fellows may scoff at some of the fizzers, but I embrace them. We all need to adapt to the changing landscape of sparkling wine.

Champagne was originally created because the winemakers had to find a way to make a pleasing wine from under-ripe grapes. Now the *vignerons* in Champagne have to train their vines and use techniques to stop their grapes achieving full ripeness, as the climate is warmer than it has ever been, a threat to the future of production. When I visited Louis Roederer champagne house I noticed some barrels in the corner of the cellar – common in the production of still wine – and asked Jean-Baptiste Lecallion (the head winemaker) if he was making still wine. He replied, 'that's my retirement project'.

Global warming is real: the climate in England is now very similar to the climate in Champagne 100 years ago when the wine became renowned. English wines feature strongly in the selection for this book. The UK has 133 wineries now; it is anything but a novelty business and the UK is creating wines that compete with and sometimes surpass the quality of our friends' wine across the Channel.

You may well recognise some of the sparkling wines featured in the book. Many of the styles have loitered on supermarket shelves for years gathering dust, biding their time before fashions change giving them the spotlight once more: moscato d'Asti and Lambrusco, sekt and even Babycham . . . yes, Babycham baby. But I hope you find some surprises too; there are wines in here from the most unlikely places which have the quality of many of the best champagne houses.

Many fizzers have been made like a champagne using the *méthode traditionnelle*, including cava, crémant, English sparkling, MCC from South Africa and many other examples. Because the production method is the same as champagne, you will find many of the same attributes in these wines, often without the price tag.

But not all sparkling wines were created equally; there are different and simpler ways of creating bubbles in wine. These methods often produce wines that are cheaper to buy, and create different styles of wines which are often easier to drink than wines made by the traditional method. Whether you are a champagne classicist or an enthusiast of the ancestral method, let the fizz flow!

OTHER METHODS

Carbonation
Literally like a soda stream, CO_2 gas is added to still wine in a pressurised tank. This method is usually for the cheap stuff. Wines made this way will go flat in your glass rather too quickly.

Ancestral method/ pétillant naturel (natural sparkling)
This method uses one fermentation instead of two, and is similar to the method used for many ciders. Wines are bottled mid-way through fermentation, so the remaining yeast eats up the last of the sugars in bottle converting it into booze and CO_2, which is captured in the bottle. This method creates wilder styles, often cloudy or with sediment, which can carry some funky animal, cidery flavours. Although these styles are on-trend right now, especially with hippest natural wine buffs, this was the first way of making sparkling wine, based on methods used by monks in Limoux in the 1500s.

TANK METHOD
(AKA: Charmat / Autoclave / *Metodo Martinotti* / *Cuvée Close*)

Charmat (Italian: *metodo Martinotti*) was developed and patented in 1895 by the Italian Federico Martinotti (1860–1924). The method was further developed with a new patent by the inventor Eugène Charmat in 1907. This process is now more often called after the French creator, which the Italians tend to dispute!

The tank method for producing sparkling wines began to be used commercially in the early twentieth century, and is mainly used for new-world fizzers, prosecco, Lambrusco and moscato wines. The major difference between the tank method and the traditional method is where the second fermentation takes place to capture the bubbles. For the traditional method, the bubbles are captured in the bottle – which is both time and labour intensive. For the tank method, the same vessel used for the first fermentation is often used to turn a still wine into a sparkling one. During the wine's second fermentation, the CO_2 released from the fermentation causes the tank to pressurise, and bubbles are dissolved back into the wine, creating sparkling wine. This new sparkling wine is then filtered, dosed with sugar and bottled without aging, ready for popping and enjoying.

Tank-method sparkling wines have a much fresher and fruitier style, rather than the toasty notes you find in bottle-fermented sparkling. This means prosecco and other tank-method sparklings reflect the fruity flavours of the grapes, rather than secondary yeasty flavours. Some narrow-minded wine professionals may argue that the tank method produces only basic styles of wine, and although there is a quality ceiling on these styles, the tank method can produce amazing examples of sparkling. Champagne needs a minimum of 15 months aging before release, which means all champagnes on the market are at least two years old before they reach the consumer. Prosecco grapes can be harvested, processed and bottled ready for drinking within 60 days of being picked. This is the major reason why prosecco or charmat-method fizzers are generally a fraction of the cost of champagne and other traditional-method sparklers. The production process is quick and efficient, which means producers can make a lot of volume quickly. The process makes these wines affordable, which is a contributing factor to the popularity of prosecco in the first place.

★ **Base Wine + Yeast** The base wine either stays inside or is placed in an autoclave or Charmat tank (a pressure-resistant tank). A mixture of selected yeast and often sugar is added to the base wine to kick start the next fermentation.

★ **Second Fermentation** Wines complete their second fermentation in the pressurised tank, letting the fermentation's by-product CO_2 gas dissolve back into the wine. This usually takes around 10 days, but some high-quality wines can take up to 60 days.

★ **Stabilising and Filtration** When the wine has successfully finished the secondary fermentation, it is almost ready. The wines are kept very cold to avoid further unwanted fermentation and are then filtered to remove yeast and sediments, which make the wine cloudy. Some more natural sparklers can be bottled without filtration.

★ **Spoonful of Sugar and Bottling** Before bottling, after filtration, the near-finished fizz is often injected with sugar or sweet grape must for the desired sugar level, i.e. brut or extra dry.

PROSECCO

Prosecco is a modern success story because of its fun, fruity and foaming nature and relatively low cost. The growth in popularity has meant the region's production has expanded quickly, from 50 million bottles in 2006 to over 400 million in 2016. No other wine in history has risen to the top of the pops so quickly! This Italian sparkling wine is produced in the regions of Veneto and Friuli-Venezia Giulia, in the north-east corner of Italy. Between the towns of Conegliano and Valdobbiadene, north of Treviso. The best proseccos are produced in these cooler hills which have calcareous and limestone soils. The climate of the region is generally warm and wet owing to the protective mountains and tepid rains of the Adriatic. Lush and green, with a rolling carpet of patchwork vines, hilltop towns and breath-taking Alpine views, the area has just attained UNESCO World Heritage status as an area of natural beauty.

Prosecco is the name of the wine, rather than the grape variety, which is 'glera'. This high-yielding fruity wee number is perfect for the cost-effective production of early-drinking sparkling wines. The first example of 'prosecco' being used to describe the wine was in 1754 by dandy Aureliano Acanti stating; 'And now I would like to wet my mouth with that Prosecco with its apple bouquet'. Almost 300 years on, prosecco's apple bouquet is the reason it sells over 400 million bottles a year.

As you would expect, the largest market for prosecco is Italy; the largest export markets are the USA and the UK. In Britain we have a rampant love affair with prosecco and are set to drink 100 million bottles a year by 2020, over a quarter of the total production. Historically it is drunk in the home region of Veneto and in the bars and piazzas of Verona and Venice, where it is famously used as a base for cocktails as well as enjoyed in its own right.

The iconic Bellini cocktail must be the most famous, invented in Venetian institution Harry's Bar in 1948. The Bellini is a prosecco poured with *succo di pesca* (fresh white peach juice). Peachy, fizzing and thickly fruity, absolutely delicious. The name Bellini is a reference to Renaissance painter Giovanni Bellini, famed for the pink hues in his work, and a similar pinkie brightness is reminiscent in the now famous drink. But other drinks have helped propel the success of prosecco. I remember my surprise on first visiting Verona, entering the enchanting Piazza delle Erbe for an Italian Wine event, to see gesticulating locals drinking what looked to be Irn Bru. On closer inspection, it was Aperol Spritz, which is prosecco and aperol (bitter aperitif with orange and cinchona) with soda and orange.

With its floral, fruity bouquet and fresh, light flavour full of pizzazz, prosecco is the ultimate simple but sophisticated wine which personifies the unique Italian lifestyle, *la dolce vita*!

Quality levels

Prosecco DOC: Made from high-yielding vines, usually from the flat fertile plains. The vast majority of all production is made within this legal perimeter.

Prosecco DOCG: Smaller yields meaning more flavourful grapes, usually grown in the hills and hand-harvested. Less than a quarter of total production is made within this higher-quality level.

Prosecco Superiore DOCG: Only a fraction of total production is made within this high-quality level. Grown in the hills between historic towns of Conegliano and Valdobbiadene, yields are smaller and all grapes must be harvested by hand. Owing to the quality-focused and labour-intensive production, expect to pay a premium.

Prosecco Superiore di [vineyard name]: This is the top level of all prosecco; it can be a delimited single vineyard, written as *Rive* on the label, from the hillsides of the Conegliano–Valdobbiadene area and must represent the best quality in the zone. Prosecco Superiore di Cartizze, which is a tiny oasis and Prosecco's oldest cru, is thought to be the 'Grand Cru' best quality in the whole region. Cartizze production represents less than 0.25% of total prosecco production.

Prosecco styles

Tranquillo: a rare find outside of the Prosecco region, this is still prosecco made with the glera grape, but these wines are only just sparkling

Frizzante: lightly sparkling, often closed with a normal flat cork. Perfect for day drinking. 1– 2.5 bar of bubbles

Spumante: fully sparkling, when only a bubbly hit will do. Must be higher than 3 bar of pressure (champagne is closer to 6 bar).

Sweetness levels

It is easy to think prosecco is sweeter than champagne; it often tastes like it. However, generally both champagne and prosecco are the same or similar sweetness levels. Prosecco can appear to taste sweeter as it's lower in astringency, acidity and fizz.

Brut: 0–9g sugar per bottle, so around a gram per glass

Extra dry: 9–12.75g sugar per bottle, but many proseccos labelled brut and extra dry overlap in sweetness. It is the producer's prerogative to decide how to label the wine, and can depend on the market.

Dry: 12.75–24g sugar per bottle. Don't ask me why, but dry prosecco is actually sweet – tastes like Appletise.

Demi-sec: 24–37.5g sugar per bottle, super sweet and very rare.

Type: Crémant du Jura, brut
Style: Tangerine Dream
Price: £
Stockists: High street
Toast:
Food: Frozen scampi and a vat of tartare sauce
Occasion: Work drinks, or catering for the masses
Website: www.aldi.co.uk

Tasting note: *Burnt butter and cut lemons, tangerines and golden deliciousness on the nose with some yeasty top notes. The palate is all fizzy white Hovis with Flora and bright appley character – think Appletise with bread sticks. The finish has an Alpine edge and ends with a racy clementine zap. Bright and moreish, this is a fine example, and credit is due to Aldi and winemaker Nicolas Haeffelin.*

52 *

ALDI EXQUISITE COLLECTION CRÉMANT DU JURA

Winner of multiple awards and boasting market-beating prices, the German discounters have changed the face of grocery retailing in the UK forever. They buy wine with German efficiency, using their economies of scale to customers' benefit; the value is stonking. I can never quite believe the prices when browsing the wine aisles. I am not saying every wine is exceptional, but there are some serious stars in the range, and this crémant from Jura is definitely one of them.

The wine region of Jura is one of France's best-kept secrets: a three-hour drive south from Champagne, next door to Burgundy in the foothills of the Alps, it creates some of the most exciting wines in the world today, particularly from local grape chardonnay. The region's cult following is mostly down to a few brilliant producers creating unusual styles of wine which are stylistically in between great white burgundy and sherry, to use a broad brush. But the crémants are also turbo.

They are created using a *méthode traditionnelle* that is exactly the same as many great blanc de blancs champagnes. 100% chardonnay, secondary bottle fermentation and extended time on lees in the cellar give the hallmark toastiness. It's difficult to believe you can buy three of these bottles for the price of one bottle of champagne. I know which most consumers would prefer.

Type: Sparkling English perry
Style: Prancing in the street
Price: £
Stockists: High street
Toast: 0
Food: Chips with cheese
Occasion: Party like it's 1999
Website: www.babycham.com

Tasting note: *Floral, fruity, sweet and fizzy. Simple and super-easy, no complexity or length, so keep drinking it!*

53*

BABYCHAM

Launched in the United Kingdom in 1953, Babycham was the first alcoholic product to be advertised on British commercial television and changed our drinking habits forever.

Cider and perry had been made in Somerset for thousands of years but the styles were never commercially produced, until Francis Showering served his 'Champagne de Poire' in local agricultural shows. It proved to be super-popular; served in baby-sized bottles, the drink was quickly coined 'baby cham', and so it was born!

Babycham skyrocketed, its popularity as much to do with marketing as the taste itself. The baby deer logo was new to alcoholic advertising, and using champagne's associations with luxury to sell cheap perry was genius. The 1960s adverts read 'The Babycham bottle fills a champagne glass!' The company even produced its own branded champagne-style coupe glasses.

Post-war Britain saw a lot of social change. Women were leading the movement and wanted something to drink other than draft bitter or port! Babycham was the taste of aspiration at the time. It represented a heady taste of the high life glimpsed only in magazines or the cinema. Over the years it rose to the heights of fame, with TV commercials and nationwide beauty contests looking for the next Babycham Babe. Nowadays it tends to be relegated to the bottom shelf of the supermarkets; my claim to fame is that I launched a 75cl version when I was wine buying at Tesco. People still prefer the small bottles, and the company sells a whopping 15 million bottles a year!

Babycham fell out of favour when other cheap, easy-drinking styles came onto the market, but it has kept its brand equity and popularity. You can link the meteoric rise in popularity of many drinks since then, including prosecco, as a direct descendant of Babycham. We have a lot to thank the little deer for!

Type: Franciacorta, brut
Style: A glacial arousal
Price: ££
Stockists: High street
Toast:
Food: White fish, broad beans and olive oily potatoes
Occasion: Pre-holiday tipple
Website: www.bellavistawine.it

Tasting note: *Loads of appeal with fresh baked loaf, apple, pears, peach and apricot juice. There is some toasty character too with a touch of marmite on seedy rye. The palate is foaming and soft, golden orchard fruit; white peaches and oranges fill and flesh out this elegant sparkler. Almost Bellini in flavour but with mineral edges and a creamy gentle finish. Bravo.*

54 *

BELLAVISTA ALMA GRAN CUVÉE

FRANCIACORTA IS A RELATIVELY YOUNG WINE REGION, FOUNDED IN the 1960s, although quality still wines have been made for a long time before this. We don't find so many examples in our stores, as the proximity of the region to the cities of Milan and Turin, and the popular holiday destination of the Italian lakes, mean most of the production is hoovered up domestically or by thirsty tourists. Do look out for these wines as they offer champagne quality, great value with a gentler fizz and a twist of the *dolce vita*.

Alma Gran Cuvée is Bellavista's flagship fizzer, and this wine represents what Bellavista is all about: exceptional franciacorta. It tastes as beautiful as the region it's from: surely one of the world's most stunning, based around the Lago d'Iseo in the foothills of the Italian Alps. Started in 1977 Bellavista has become one of the most desirable franciacortas, for its consistent quality wines and stylish bottle design, the full Italian package.

The vines are grown on south-facing exposure, to soak up maximum sunlight hours tempered by cold alpine breezes. Only the old vines go into the Alma Gran Cuvée, yielding the most flavoursome fruit. The grapes are similar to those used in champagne, predominately chardonnay, pinot noir and an aromatic seasoning of pinot blanc, and fermentation is by the *méthode traditionnelle* for franciacorta, the same as for champagne. Clever use of neutral oak barrel and extended ageing on lees add further creaminess and spice to this elegant beauty.

Type: Canadian, brut, vintage
Style: Atlantic refreshment
Price: £££
Stockists: Specialist
Toast: 🍞🍞🍞
Food: Poutine obvs
Occasion: Trudeau state visit
Website: www.benjaminbridge.com

Tasting note: *As fresh as the arctic wind, as foamy as the stormy Atlantic and as delicious as a fat stack of Canadian pancakes lathered in maple syrup. Creamy and taught on the palate, with green apple freshness which keeps the wine achingly fresh. Gorgeous stone fruit and fizzy Haribo citrus, framed by Canadian-toast-like complexity, rich and refreshing giving waves of enjoyment. Watch out Champagne, Canada is catching up.*

55*

BENJAMIN BRIDGE MÉTHODE CLASSIQUE BRUT 2012

OFF THE BLOCK BENJAMIN BRIDGE HAS BEEN MAKING BIG WAVES with their high-punching fizz since 2002, which are now hitting our UK shores. Fiercely Nova Scotian, Benjamin Bridge company is based in the rural heart of the Gaspereau Valley, east-coast Canada. This unusual place for viticulture has made the wine world take notice of the quality potential of this cool-climate wine area. By cool climate I mean it's bloody freezing: temperatures can drop to –28°C during the winter months; snow is frequent. But the proximity to the open Atlantic does have a mediating effect, and the climate through the vine-growing season isn't too dissimilar to Champagne or the south of England.

In early 2018, Benjamin Bridge invited many of the UK wine press and London's top *somms* to a private tasting. The catch was that the wines were blind; unknown to the tasters the wines served were a mixture of top Grande Marque champagne and Benjamin Bridge fizzers.

The experts had to submit their scores and results were tallied up: 80% of the wine experts preferred the sparkling wines from Nova Scotia. This either means wine experts are full of shit, or BB's wines are the mutt's nuts. In this case both are true.

The Brut 2012 is a classical champagne blend from BB's organic vines of chardonnay, pinot noir and pinot meunier. The base wines have seen 10% of oak barrel, which gives more creaminess on the palate. The Brut develops further delicious flavours while it rests on lees for a whopping four years. The results speak for themselves; this is better than a lot of champagne – plus Trudeau is a dude.

Type: Franciacorta, brut, vintage
Style: The finest Italian silk
Price: ££££
Stockists: Specialist
Toast: 🍞🍞🍞
Food: Risotto bianca, or pork chops dripping in burnt butter
Occasion: Fashion Week
Website: www.berlucchi.it

Tasting note: *Lavish, softly foaming with a delicate, fine and golden caress. Filled with yellow gemstones, jewels of white peaches and exotic fruit flavours. There is an undercurrent of toasted spice, creamy macchiato resting on flavours of grilled ciabatta. The gentle sparkle means it is rather too easy to drink, so be warned as this is liquid dolce vita!*

56*

BERLUCCHI PALAZZO LANA SATÈN FRANCIACORTA RISERVA 2008

ALTHOUGH FRANCIACORTA IS RELATIVELY UNKNOWN OUTSIDE OF Italy, I hope many of the prosecco die-hards upgrade their fizz habits to franciacorta, which offers more complexity and finesse when the time is right.

Local winemaker Franco Ziliani and aristocratic landowner Guido Berlucchi joined forces in 1955. Ziliani was spellbound by the potential in the land, the regal palace of Palazzo Lana Berlucchi and its ancient underground cellars. Ziliani's dream was to produce champagne-style wines in his local area, a wine region historically dedicated to still table wines. It was a punchy move! But it paved the future of franciacorta.

Berlucchi is now a household name in Italy; the wine is mostly sunk in the bars and trattorias of glitzy Milano but a few bottles are exported, and the company has plans to expand this.

The Palazzo Lana Satèn 2008 Franciacorta Riserva is Berlucchi's top expression. Satèn must be a blanc de blancs, in this case 100% chardonnay, but you do find examples made from pinot blanc. It also dictates a lighter pressure bar: although very sparkling, it is less fizzy and aggressive than many champagnes – and will be preferred by many.

Once the free-run juice is fermented in the autumn the base wine stays in oak barrels for six months, giving extra weight and creamy complexity. In the spring a vigorous taste selection is made, making sure only the top wines make the cut for Palazzo Lana. The wine spends seven years on lees in the cellars, giving this wine mega toast flavours, while retaining all the stylish, fresh-faced grace of the best of the Franciacorta region.

Type: Crémant de Limoux, brut, multi-vintage,
Style: Opal Fruits and Angel Delight
Price: £
Stockists: Berry Bros. & Rudd
Toast:
Food: Chicken Caesar
Occasion: Garden Party
Website: www.bbr.com

Tasting note: *Sunshine fills the glass and wafts out with ripe lemons, cut melons and chardonnay-style fruit flavours. There is a delicious toasty character of hot cross buns and a pinch of something a little floral. Soft, foaming and very drinkable, this is a high-class fizz from wine trade royalty.*

57*

BERRY BROS. & RUDD CRÉMANT DE LIMOUX

IN THE MOUNTAIN-LOCKED TOWN OF LIMOUX IN THE LANGUEDOC, the locals have been making sparkling wine longer than anywhere else in the world. The first written mention of the local sparkling wine, Blanquette de Limoux, was in 1531, but it's likely the wines had been made for a long time before this in the Benedictine Abbey of Saint-Hilaire. This was years before Dom Pérignon was even born, and many believe Limoux inspired the wines of champagne in the first place.

Based in the historical cellars in St James in central London, Berry has been providing fine wines to the world's richest and most discerning wine drinkers for centuries, but has redefined itself in recent years. Still a benchmark for quality and style, Berry only works with the best wineries from around the world. Its own-label selection has won many awards, and is terrific value – not a word you often associate with the most famous wine merchant in the world. Lucky for us.

Berry's Crémant de Limoux was created by legendary Simon Fields, Master of Wine, and family-owned Antech, the most prestigious producer in Limoux. Beside the fortified town of Carcassonne, the hilly vineyards of Limoux lead on to ancient forests with a snow-capped backdrop of the Pyrenees. Winemaker Francoise is sixth-generation and creates expressive sparkling wines using ancient and modern practices.

A blend of 70% chardonnay with a dollop of chenin blanc and local mauzac, this perfect quaffing fizz is aged on lees, just like a champagne. Because of the blend and the sunshine of the south of France, this fizz is softer, more populous and all together easier to drink than many champagnes. There aren't many examples of better-value fizz.

Type: Californian, *pétillant naturel*, vintage
Style: Dancing on yellow plum sponge
Price: ££
Stockists: Specialist
Toast:
Food: Sloppy Giuseppe or gooseneck barnacles
Occasion: The end of a hard day's graft
Website: https://birichino.vinespring.com

Tasting note: Greeny yellow in appearance, like homemade lemonade. The nose is all cream soda, Mountain Dew, jasmine and pithy pink grapefruit, inviting and super-fun. The palate flirts and foams, tickling your taste buds with titillating flavours of yellow plums, sour grapes and lemon drizzle cup cakes.

58*

BIRICHINO 2017 PÉTULANT NATUREL MALVASIA BIANCA

ALEX KRAUSE AND JOHN LOCKE FOUNDED BIRICHINO WINERY IN 2008 and since then they have a built a worldwide cult following for their exotic styles from the Californian coast. Between the duo, they have 40 years of winemaking experience, working with some of the greatest producers in native California and around the world. Now, the pair are letting their hair down allowing their creative juices to flow in Santa Cruz. Their full range of wines is awesome: their old-vine red wines are worth looking out, but I'm here to gush lyrical about bubbles. Their *pétillant naturel* (Pét-Nat) is to die for. And, out of all the 101 wines featured here, this is the only one to be bottled in a car park.

All great wines challenge the drinker in one way or another: at Birichino, their aim is to excite people's palates. Their vinification leans towards minimal intervention; they use wild fermentations and avoid filtration, which means you get the raw taste and true personality of their vineyards and grapes.

The Malvasia Bianca grape produces aromatic wines, with floral charms and winegum-like flavours; it is not a classic sparkling grape variety. This would be a rogue move anywhere other than California, but here they love innovation. This wine doesn't explore new styles, unlike many others in this book. During the base wine fermentation, some of the juice is held back and added to the wine at the time of bottling – in the nearby parking lot. The results are lightly sparkling fruit bomb, with a cloudy apple juice appearance. This haze is from the fine lees which remain in bottle (in champagne these are removed at disgorgement). These lees give a creaminess to the palate and a subtle burger bun toastiness. Anything but petulant, this wine will only put a beaming grin on your face.

Type: English sparkling, brut
Style: This is England
Price: ££
Stockists: High street
Toast:
Food: Cockles and mussels, alive, alive oh!
Occasion: Seaside brunch with your besties
Website: www.breakybottom.co.uk/

Tasting note: *Toasty floral nose, hot cross buns and hedgerow, yeasty notes but more citrus, lemon drizzle cake and sour cream, razor fresh with a saline oyster and margarita character. Foaming palate, a bit grassy, nice toasted fruit and distinctly English Bramley apple acidity.*

59 *

BREAKY BOTTOM BRUT 2013 SEYVAL BLANC CUVÉE SIR HARRY KROTO

A PIONEER IN THE UK WINE SCENE, PETER HALL PLANTED HIS BREAKY Bottom vineyard in 1974. It is a secluded farm in a beautiful valley in the South Downs near Lewes. The vineyards share the land with a flock of 40 ewes, who graze the surrounding steep hillsides. Harsh winters aren't often associated with the south of England, but because of the rural setting of Breaky Bottom, Peter has even been snowed in over the years, although he should have had enough wine and lamb to keep him going.

Peter makes *méthode traditionnelle* sparkling from the usual suspects: chardonnay, pinot noir and pinot meunier. But he became famous for a different set of grape varieties, huxelrebe, reichensteiner and seyval blanc. These grapes used to be more common in the UK as they were chosen for their vigour and yields in our cold and wet climate, rather than the high quality of the wines they produce. These Germanic or hybrid varieties are a dying breed in the UK, but seyval blanc produces successful styles of still and sparkling wine and there is no better sparkling example than Peter's.

Peter named this wine after a good friend who died in 2017; Sir Harry Kroto was a Nobel Prize winning scientist. The Seyval Blanc 2013 is a delight, and a nod to the original styles of English wine, before bigger budgets and champagne chasers started to dominate production here. This is a pure taste of England, provoking thoughts of hot cross buns, spring meadows and bleating lambs bopping across the East Sussex Downs.

Type: English sparkling rosé, brut, vintage
Style: Strawberries with Cornish cream dream
Price: £££
Stockists: High street
Toast:
Food: High tea with Granny
Occasion: Overdue catch-ups
Website: www.camelvalley.com

Tasting note: *English strawberries and cream, notes of wild strawberries and bright raspberries fill the nose. The palate is pretty in pink, more wild berries, a crack of spice, Cornish cream mousse with a touch of scone with a long and whooshing finish.*

60*

CAMEL VALLEY PINOT NOIR ROSÉ BRUT 2015

CAMEL VALLEY, FOUNDED BY BOB LINDO IN 1989, IS 100% FAMILY run in the idyllic Cornish countryside. The company produces a range of cracking still wines and sparklers. They are one of the furthest west producers in the UK and have a range of wines which are dripping with awards and quality recognition. This rosé, in the 2009 vintage, was crowed Sparking Rosé World Champion ahead of many famous champagnes. British Airways serve Camel Valley wines in first class, and Buckingham Palace are avid fans. In March 2018, Bob was the first British wine producer to receive a royal warrant, joining an elite club: Bollinger, Pol Roger and Pimm's – the royals generally have good taste. Ever since he has had to turn large customers away, including some very reputable store chains who are queuing up for his wine!

Camel Valley was also the first English producer to receive a 'Protected Designation Origin' from the EU for one of their vineyards. This is a legal perimeter for quality produce, delimiting the area of production, like all the important wine regions in Europe. This type of law will inevitably spread to all English producers, protecting quality, adding bureaucracy, avoiding any harmful production methods and unifying regionality.

The company has become very famous for the quality of its rosé in recent years. For the 2015 vintage, the pinot noir grapes were crushed lightly to keep the delicate, crunchy fruit characters of the Cornish grapes. Camel Valley uses only free-run juice for the sparkling wine, what the French call *tête de cuvée*, which is the highest-quality juice. Spending 12 months on lees gives this wine a wonderful toasty edge, but the fruit flavours dominate, resulting in more strawberry dreams for the drinker.

Type: Brazilian sparkler, vintage
Style: Steel drum rhythm
Price: ££
Stockists: Specialist
Toast: ▢▢▢
Occasion: Carnival!
Food: Fish tacos with lime and mango
Website: www.cavegeisse.com.br

Tasting note: *White fruit, jungle boogie, earthy and foaming. Toasted nuts, white bread and Umbongo juice fill the floral and seamless palate. Fizzy, novel and down-the-hatch delicious.*

61*

CAVE GEISSE BLANC DE BLANC 2012

I WAS FIRST INTRODUCED TO CAVE GEISSE WHEN I WAS ON A WINE-buying trip to Chile, visiting Casa Silva, a top-quality producer south of Santiago, who gave me the tip off. I'm pleased they did. Their winemaking consultant, Mario Geisse, was making premium fizz on the other side of the Andes. Cave Geisse is already hugely reputable in South America and it won't be long before we find Mario's Brazilian sparklers filling up our shelves.

The Geisse Winery was founded in 1979 by winemaker Mario Geisse, a Chilean who moved to Brazil in 1976 to direct Moët & Chandon's sparkling operation. Big job, and although he was head of a multinational team creating big volumes of premium wines, he quickly realised the untapped quality potential of the Pinto Bandeira region. He left his famous employer to embark on his own project to unlock the quality he so adamantly believed in, and ever since has been pioneering quality fizz and still wines across Brazil.

In the region of Bento Gonçalves in the south of Brazil, he found the perfect spot for the creation of top-end fizz, at an altitude of 800m on ancient basaltic and volcanic soils that offer both excellent drainage and important mineral characteristics on the finished wine.

100% chardonnay with a minimum ageing time of 36 months on lees mean this Brazilian wine is developing beautiful evolution in the bottle now. Brut – the residual sugar is around 6 grams per bottle – it offers an exotic alternative to your usual favourite fizzer.

Type: English sparkling, brut, vintage
Style: Tailored tweed tuxedo
Price: ££££
Stockists: High street
Toast:
Food: Halibut with lemons and samphire
Occasion: Next season of *Game of Thrones*
Website: www.chapeldown.com

Tasting note: The nose is all green apple, cool orchard fruit, hedgerow, touch of bread and sweet gorse. The palate shows affable toasty notes of fresh muffins and bags of freshly cut apples and pears, fresh and twangy. Toast and spice are there, as is minerality on the long and foaming finish.

62 *

CHAPEL DOWN KIT'S COTY BLANC DE BLANCS 2013

CHAPEL DOWN BASED IN TENTERDEN IN KENT HAVE BUILT A STRONG reputation for quality English wines. Their still wine Bacchus Reserve is probably the best still wine in the UK. I'm particularly fond of their top-drawer beer Curious Brew, which is fermented using champagne yeasts. After a day of tasting wine, beer is often the only answer.

The company has built up a great customer base over recent years; the wines are readily available in Waitrose, the Gordon Ramsay group and often served at No.10 Downing Street. It was the first English wine producer to be listed on the London Stock Exchange; evidently there is a lot of investment and clever strategy behind the fizzy facade.

This is their first new release in some time, and it's aiming towards the prestige cuvée end of the market. The single Kit's Coty vineyard is a massive plot of 95 acres, based on rolling hills of the North Downs of Kent. The vineyard is south facing, as all the best vineyards are in England, benefiting from maximum sunlight hours during the day; and the free-draining chalk soils provide the perfect *terroir*. Capped yields and careful selection mean Chapel Down winemaker Josh Donaghay-Spire can showcase these qualities in his wines.

This blanc de blancs was harvested by hand in October, then followed classic *méthode traditionnelle* winemaking. 2013 was a sunny enough summer and the vineyard produced great chardonnay grapes: 20% of the blend is matured in barrel, giving additional body and complexity to the finished wine. Time is English sparkling wine's greatest asset, and this example has had three years on lees before release. The result is impressive, and gives many champagne blanc de blancs a run for their money.

Type: Lambrusco
Style: Sour cherry hit
Price: ££
Stockists: Specialist
Toast: 0
Food: Tortellini in brodo, barbeque or plates of parma ham
Occasion: Lunch
Website: www.chiarli.it

Tasting note: *Bright pink, foaming and tutti frutti on the nose, inviting with funfair bootlaces and raspberry freshness. The palate is delicately foaming, packed with sour cherry, wild strawberry and redcurrant character and a lip-puckering acidity. Dry, with a lick of tannin, this is beautiful chilled but does benefit from the accompaniment of a plate of pasta.*

63*

CLETO CHIARLI E FIGLI VECCHIA MODENA PREMIUM

LAMBRUSCO HAS AN UNJUST REP IN THE UK, AND I'LL TELL YOU WHY. In the 1970s and 1980s, a style of lambrusco was invented for the UK market. Light in booze at 5%, cheap as chips, sweet, fizzy and Italian (sound familiar?), it was super-popular. So much so that some drinks manufacturers in the UK wanted a slice of the pie for themselves – and *voilà*: the lambrusco rip-off lambrini was born. Made from pears in a factory outside Liverpool, it was an overnight success. Now lambrini out sells lambrusco by a 1000 to 1. But the Lambrini Girls have had their day, it's lambrusco's time to shine.

This is one of the most famous lambruscos from Modena, in the heartland of Emilia Romagna, which has some of the best cuisine in Italy. Since 1860, Chiarli has been producing everyday wines, which offer quality affordable enjoyment.

Like all great wines, it comes in many styles and colours; the Vecchia Modena is pure lambrusco, the original, the best. The style has changed slightly over the years, but the label has remained the same since its launch in 1892 and today is considered an icon of the region.

From a single vineyard on the fertile plains to the south of Modena, the wine is made from 100% lambrusco di Sorbara grape, hand-harvested and lightly pressed. 24 hours on skins means it has a vivid Vimto colour, almost luminous. Made in the charmat method, similar to prosecco, this lambrusco is delicately sparking and a lunchtime-light 11% in alcohol, perfect for day drinking or a session. Unlike a lot of the cheap and bottom-shelf examples, this isn't sweet but contains 6 grams of sugar per bottle, which gives it a dry and pretty serious character that definitely shows best with food. Chin chin!

Type: New Zealand sparkling wine, multi-vintage
Style: Kiwi fizz, French polish
Price: ££
Stockists: High street
Toast: 🍞🍞🍞
Food: Crab cakes and green papaya salad
Occasion: All Blacks vs anyone in the autumn internationals
Website: www.cloudybay.co.nz

Tasting note: *Crisp apples, white flowers, medley of citrus and toasty notes on the nose, the palate is as fresh as glacial melt, with flavours of cut green apples, crunchy berries and lemon twang framed by an open toasty character of brioche.*

64*

CLOUDY BAY PELORUS

THE CLOUDY BAY WINERY WAS NAMED AFTER A BODY OF WATER CLOSE to Marlborough that Captain James Cook came across during his voyage to New Zealand in 1770. Two hundred years later Cloudy Bay winery was established in 1985, and was one of the first wineries to venture into Marlborough, when it was almost an unthinkable place to plant a vineyard. But Cloudy Bay's founder, David Hohnen, saw huge potential in the region to produce great wines, and invested to secure the best land in the area. Over the years, Marlborough has risen to wine world fame and New Zealand's leading wine region, producing some of the best and most popular styles on the planet, particularly sauvignon blanc.

As part of the global luxury goods firm LVMH, which also owns Veuve Clicquot, Dom Pérignon and Krug among others, Cloudy Bay has a lot of expertise in producing top-end sparkling. Using its fizzy skillset, it has been making fantastic *méthode traditionnelle* sparkling for years, known as Pelorus.

It is a champagne-style blend of chardonnay and pinot noir grapes, sourced from a combination of vineyards located within the Wairau Valley, from free-draining gravel-based soils which give plump and fruity grapes. The chardonnay and pinot noir are inoculated with a Burgundian Montrachet yeast, and the base wines are fermented in a mixture of steel tanks, small French barrels and large oak vats, giving winemaker Tim Heath as much diversity as possible to play with in creating the blends. After two years on lees, the Pelorus has built up tasty toastiness and lovely foaming mousse. Dosed at 6 grams of sugar per bottle, analytically it is very similar to champagne, but is a taste of the open skies of New Zealand, with a distinctive French polish.

Type: Cava, brut, vintage
Style: Dead-good cava
Price: £££
Stockists: Specialist
Toast: 🍞🍞
Food: Mixed seafood paella, or sushi
Occasion: Spain vs France in the Euros
Website: http://arscollectacodorniu.com

Tasting note: *Straw yellow with golden flashes, the nose is filled by fruity notes of red cherries, raspberry and red spices, red peppers and paprika. The palate is more evolved, showing the extended time on lees, a complex mix of red, gold fruit, cupboard spice rack and toasty, bready character. The foam is elegant and there is a marked minerality on the finish.*

65*

CODORNÍU FINCA EL TROS NOU 2009

You will have probably heard of Codorníu; it makes a lot of cava. The family are paramount to the history and success of the wider Cava region and have an impressive winemaking history, dating all the way back to 1551. The entry-level fizz is widely available, and priced well under £10 a bottle, a good value example of what cava can be. The top levels of Codorníu's range are exciting, none more so than their single-vineyard El Tros Nou. This single plot of vines, or *paraje*, is located in one of the coldest zones of the Cava, the Sierra de Prades, at above 550 metres altitude. The cool climate, paired with the special Llicorella slate soils, give the pinot noir a real sense of place, which is rare and welcomed in Cava.

The *paraje* was planted in 1985, so the vines have had over 30 years to dig deep into the poor, slatey soils giving minerality and personality to the finished wine. Harvesting at night keeps the grapes cool, retaining the delicate fresh fruit flavours of the pinot noir. Considering the industrial scale of Codorníu, El Tros Nou was created in an artisanal way. All hand-harvested, with fermentation carried out in small oak vats, endeavouring to keep as much personality in the wines as possible. Made in a blanc de noirs style, it is rested on lees for ages, 90 months, building big toasty flavours in Codorníu's most historic cellar. Dosage, at just above 9 grams of sugar a bottle, gives a similar sweetness to a lot of brut champagne but offers a lot more complexity than many of the Frenchies. *Vamos*!

Type: Nebbiolo d'Alba spumante
Style: Tickled pink
Price: ££
Stockists: Specialist
Toast:
Food: Carpaccio or tuna steaks
Occasion: Bank holiday
Website: http://cuvage.it/en

Tasting note: *Very pale pink, raspberry and peppery on the nose, with a touch of sour berries. The palate is a relentless cascade of raspberry and strawberry, creamy and pleasing. Commercial rather than complex, which is a joy to drink. Nice definition to the palate, with top notes of violets and rose petals, some gleaming Nebbiolo character framed by a touch of biscotti biscuit.*

66*

CUVAGE ROSATO

THE NORTH-WEST CORNER OF ITALY IS ONE OF THE MOST FAMOUS REGIONS for culture and gastronomic delights: the Slow Food movement, Turin, Juventus, white truffles, the regal wines of Barolo and now the elegant sparkling wines of the Alte Langhe region.

Cuvage is the foremost producer of these champagne-styled fizzers, a venture by the Martini family (not the same family as the Vermouth) who make some of the best-selling Italian wine in the UK, including prosecco. Their world-class winemakers know a thing or two about good bubbles. The state-of-the art winery came into being after the *terroir*, and local nebbiolo grape, were identified for the production of top-shelf sparkling. Many experts see the parallels between nebbiolo and pinot noir – one of the principal grapes in Champagne.

The area where this grape grows is one of the most beautiful in the world, and the region of Barolo was recently named as a UNESCO heritage site for its natural beauty. The name of the grape nebbiolo derives from the fog (or *nebbia*) of the mountain-locked area, which produces delicate looking grapes with powerful personality. When the fog clears (which is a rarity!) you have 180 degrees of jagged white alps, rolling landscapes of vineyards, broken by medieval spires and towns perched on hilltops.

The grapes for this fizzer grow between the towns of Vergne and Barolo, 380–450 metres above sea level. This altitude retains freshness and purity in the grapes, which translate into cleansing and racy styles of sparkling, showcasing the crunchy and floral qualities of nebbiolo. Twenty-four months resting on lees in the Cuvage cellars give this rosato a wonderful creaminess and dangerous drinkability. Expect to see more and more Cuvage in the future.

Type: Crémant, multi-vintage
Style: Savage and sensual
Price: ££
Stockists: High street
Toast:
Food: Beetroot and goats' cheese
Occasion: Engagement lunch with your mum
Website: www.domainebreton.net

Tasting note: *Mineral and creamy, with taut chalky, green-apple acidity softened by notes of jasmine, white flowers and wild honey dripping on freshly baked baguette. It will cellar well for a few years, but I think this Dabbler is best drunk ASAP in the sunshine.*

67*

DOMAINE BRETON LA DILETTANTE MÉTHODE TRADITIONNELLE

CATHERINE AND PIERRE BRETON ARE PRODUCERS OF SOME OF THE MOST personable wines from the Loire Valley. They make a host of amazing reds and whites from local grape varieties which please and delight, and Catherine's arty labels are a hit in the natural wine bars across Paris, London and beyond.

The Bretons farm 11 hectares of vines just east of Bourgueil, creating honest wines for early drinking and for cellaring. Their proudly biodynamic approach in a region and climate that is difficult for organic farming has established them as icons in the natural wine movement, since they first introduced biodynamic farming practices in 1994.

Their wines are primarily crunchy reds made from cabernet franc, known locally as 'Breton' and small quantities of chenin blanc for their vouvray, including my choice fizzer. Husband Pierre is head winemaker, and wife Catherine makes a series of cuvées under the label 'La Dilettante', or the Dabbler.

This shows how brilliant the farming and winemaking is at Domaine Breton: although the wines are totally natural and unadulterated, they are incredibly consistent, clean and utterly delicious. The Vouvray La Dilettante is slightly sparkling, dry, with a pure typicity of these old vineyards. This special fizzer comes from 50-year-old chenin blanc vines, which give amazingly flavoured grapes from their flinty soils. Made using *méthode traditionnelle*, you can expect some lovely toasty characters is this wine, and the use of indigenous yeasts and low (sometimes no) sulphur mean the wines can carry a touch of a funky character, cider-esque, adding complexity and enjoyment to this frothy dancer.

Type: Spumante, brut
Style: A titillating taste of Tuscany
Price: £££££
Stockists: Specialist
Toast: 🍞🍞🍞🍞
Food: Ravioli with crumbed fennel sausage and saffron
Occasion: Road trip
Website: www.casale-falchini.it

Tasting note: *Peachy fruit and curry-like spice, bloody delicious! The sweetness of fruit on the nose is inviting, lots of wild spices and honey. The palate is round and toasty, with burnt glazed buns, some garden herbs, citrus fruit and a marked, saline minerality typical of the Vernaccia grape from the area. The finish is creamy and foaming.*

68 *

FALCHINI SPUMANTE METODO CLASSICO

THE FALCHINI FAMILY CAN TRACE THEIR ANCESTORS BACK TO THE Medicis of Florence. Their winery, Casale Falchini, sits on the slopes below the awe-inspiring Tuscan town of towers, San Gimignano. The area was famous for the production of quality wines from Etruscan times. The white wines from local grape Vernaccia were the height of desirability during the Renaissance and are still known as some of the best in Italy. But it's the altitude and particularly the soils that make San Gimignano so special.

You can still walk through the vineyards around San Gimignano and find sea shells, although it's now 100km from the nearest sea. The abundance of shells and marine deposits in the yellow clay soil give the white wines great character. Although the area hasn't been under the sea for millions of years, there is still a saltiness to the wines here. These special soils aren't so different to a lot of Champagne's and give a similar minerality and definition to the wines.

Brothers Michael and Christopher Falchini are a winning duo, and share the work between vineyard, winery and their busy construction company. Based on the 2008 vintage, the Spumante Metodo Classico is a scrumptious blend of Vernaccia with a splash of chardonnay and pinot noir. A small proportion spends time in oak barrel, giving it even more spice and weight on the palate. It has spent nine years resting on lees in the Falchini winery – a similar time to many champagne houses' top cuvées. This extended time gives it rich biscotti-like toastiness. Only 6,600 bottles were produced of this rare Vernaccia, but it is worth searching for and is a taste of the unique.

Type: Durello spumante DOC, vintage
Style: Dive into crystal Alpine pools of toffee
Price: £££
Stockists: Specialist
Toast: 🍞🍞🍞🍞
Food: Risotto with radicchio
Occasion: Completed your tax return
Website: www.fattoriwines.com

Tasting note: *Bright with golden highlights, all secondary and tertiary on the nose – golden apple, gingerbread, Christmas cake and buttery toast. The bubbles are soft and gentle, the fruit is lean and super-dry bordering on green-apple and gooseberry tartness and this is balanced by a palate of creamy weight and nutty flavour. Herbal notes framed by an oozing, creamy texture and rounded by an oxidative panettone character. The finish is razor fresh and long.*

69*

FATTORI 2010 RONCÀ 60 MESI DURELLO DOC

ANTONIO FATTORI IS A LEGEND, HEAD-STRONG AND SUPER-PASSIONATE, from a long lineage of Antonios but the first to be professionally trained as a winemaker. His grandfather started the winery, which sits high above the volcanic hills to the north of Verona. His main focus is soave and amarone wines, which are some of the best in the region, but he also produces some top sweeties, and sparkling.

The Durello grape is local to Venezia and doesn't often travel far outside of the region, as it is usually overshadowed by the other local fizzers, including the juggernaut prosecco or nearby trento DOC. Its floral lightness and natural high acidity make it ideal for the production of top-quality fizz, and Antonio's Durello, made in a *méthode traditionnelle* (*metodo classico*) is a first-class example.

Made from grapes grown on the volcanic hills of Monte Calvarina, this fizzer displays both sense of place and lots of toasty notes from the extended time on lees, 60 months no less. There is no added sugar so it is wonderfully refreshing. If you are searching for something a little different and like your fizzers fresh and toasty, look no further.

Type: Sparkling trento DOC
Style: A race for Rapunzel's golden locks
Price: £££
Stockists: High street
Toast:
Food: Bean stew with polenta
Occasion: Italy qualifying for the World Cup, after their shocker in 2017
Website: www.ferraritrento.it

Tasting note: *Soft golden beads of finely tuned bubbles race to deliver aromas of ripe apple, mandarin peel and yellow flowers which give way to freshly baked bread lathered in salted butter sprinkled with toasted hazelnuts. Expansive, balanced and pure with a full-throttle finish of candied apple and gushing minerality.*

70*

FERRARI PERLÉ 2011 TRENTO DOC

THERE ARE TWO FAMOUS FERRARI DYNASTIES IN ITALY, BOTH FAMOUS for quality, craftsmanship and style. This Ferrari company runs on bottled luxury rather than horsepower but both are embedded in Italian culture and can knock you back into your seat. Based in Trento, lodged in the Italian Alps, Ferrari is one of the largest, and most famous, sparkling wine producers in Italy.

The company was started back in 1902 by Giulio Ferrari, who believed his home valley could produce better wines than Champagne. He was one of the first to plant substantial vineyards of chardonnay, to the horror of his neighbours. Without lineage, Giulio passed on the company to friend and local wine shop owner Bruno Lunelli in 1952, who grew the company to what it is today, and the company is now run by his extended family.

Ferrari Perlé is the top expression of the Ferrari range and has wowed the wine world ever since its first release in 1971. Since its introduction it has been crowned the Best Sparkling in the World on multiple occasions. Considering its price, which is in line with most multi-vintage champagnes, and quality on a par with many prestige cuvées, this is a top taste for an absolute bargain.

The Ferrari Perlé is a vintage blanc de blancs, made exclusively from hand-picked chardonnay grapes from the original Lunelli family vineyards located in the highest alpine slopes of the Trento valley. A minimum of five years on the lees gives amazing softness of fizz and delicious apple crumble with home-made zabaione flavours. It might be some time before I drive my own F50, but given the right occasion, a taste of Ferrari is equally exhilarating.

Type: Cava, brut, vintage
Style: Sapid silver surfer
Price: £££
Stockists: Specialist
Toast:
Food: Tapas obvs
Occasion: Drinking to forget the week
Website: www.gramona.com

Tasting note: *Evolving dried apricots, roasted cashews, camomile tea, Christmas cake spices and ginger beer. The palate is super-dry, flavours of lemon pith, a nutty evolution and steely train-track acidity.*

71*

GRAMONA ARGENT GRAN RESERVA BRUT 2009

GRAMONA, OFTEN CONSIDERED TO BE THE FINEST OF ALL CAVA HOUSES, produces great fizz. Forget the rank, earthy, rubber-band-tasting mass-market stuff: this Gran Reserva Brut will change your impressions of cava forever.

Brothers Jaume and Xavier Gramona are the fifth generation of this family business, and have set the benchmark of how good cava can be. Like the generations before them, the two brothers have taken full advantage of the best location and *terroir* of the Alt Penedès region, around 30 kilometres south of Barcelona.

They farm organic and biodynamic vineyards which produce smaller yields of flavourful grapes from steep rocky soils. In the winery they give their wines extensive ageing on lees and low levels of sugar – a trend which is now in full swing in champagne – and produce spellbinding results. Cavas are made and aged just like champagne, but only the best cavas are of parallel quality to their French counterparts. The Gramona brothers produce wines that are head and shoulders above their competitors and are one of the few producers in Cava to rival those in Champagne. Their top wines are some of the most expensive in Spain, and the Argent offers you a taste of the range, without having to sacrifice your summer holiday.

This wine is 100% chardonnay, aged on lees for a whacking 48 months, longer than required for a Gran Reserva according to the cava regulations. Dosed with under 5 grams of sugar per bottle, the finished style is as sleek as a Zara window display. A toasty, creamy, fizzing Spanish miracle.

Type: English sparkling, brut, vintage
Style: Lashings of lemon curd
Price: ££
Stockists: High street
Toast: 🍞🍞🍞
Food: Scampi, peas and curly fries
Occasion: Deleting your Facebook
Website: www.gusbourne.com

Tasting note: *Toast on the nose with real depth and some brown honey tones, top notes of fruit and hedgerow. The mouth is earthy with flavours of cherry flesh and spiced apple, brushed with cinnamon. Full and creamy, foaming and textural, a clever style which will develop in bottle. Some under-ripe fruit notes giving spikey freshness, and some riper fruit characters. Lovely toasted notes: think English muffin and lemon curd, charred from the Aga, darling.*

72 *

GUSBOURNE BRUT RESERVE 2013

GUSBOURNE LAUNCHED ITS DEBUT BRUT RESERVE VINTAGE 2006 IN 2010 and has rapidly become one of the stars of the English wine industry. Its approach to wines, branding and customer journey is one of the smartest in the UK and rivals any of the top champagne houses and wineries around the world. Based in Appledor in Kent, winemaker Charlie Holland produces some of the best sparkling in the UK, and also some rather good still wines which are as rare as hens' teeth.

The Brut Reserve is their flagship and best-selling wine, a classical blend of the three champagne grapes with chardonnay providing the dominant component, which gives the wine structure and longevity. With 28 months on lees, these are some of the toastier styles from the UK, which I love. Charlie uses a touch of oak for his wines, which aids mouthfeel, spice and complexity.

The Gusbourne vineyards, which are some of the largest in the country, are predominantly south facing, which in a cool-climate region like England has a huge benefit for the vineyards as the vines have all day to soak up precious sun and light, photosynthesising to ripeness and flavour. Charlie's touch in the winery is low intervention and clever, and he is quickly building a reputation as one of the brightest winemakers in England. The wines are so good in fact that Berry Bros. & Rudd work with Gusbourne for its own-label sparkler, cementing that it's difficult to find better quality in the UK.

Type: English sparkling, brut, multi-vintage
Style: Discerning deliciousness
Price: £££
Stockists: High street
Toast:
Food: Salt-baked cod with lemon and proper good olive oil
Occasion: Surviving Christmas
Website: www.hambledonvineyard.co.uk

Tasting note: *Top notes of an English spring garden, hedgerow, sweet magnolia and gorse in flower. A beaut toasty character to it, sort of charred sourdough pizza crust, cox apples and forest fruits. The palate is foaming with character, more crunchy apples, ripe citrus and tension of the chalk terroir with mouth-watering purity. Delish.*

73*

HAMBLEDON CLASSIC CUVÉE

THERE IS A LOT TO SAY ABOUT HAMBLEDON. WITHOUT A DOUBT IN THE top three producers in England today, creating wines from their thoroughbred chalk vineyards in Hampshire. The company and vineyards have gone through a lot of changes since the first vines were planted in 1952 with the help of Pol Roger. They led the new wave of English wine producers but because of various factors, the winery was almost mothballed and by the mid 1990s, all the grapes were sold off to other wineries.

But then Ian Kellet gave Hambledon its due renaissance. He purchased the farm in 1999, and after studying at Plumpton College in East Sussex (I'm a fellow alumnus), he has been on a mission to restore and surpass its former glory. So far it's working out pretty well.

Ian has hired a team of Champenois in the vineyards and cellars with the renowned Hervé Jestin at the helm. Hervé is probably the best winemaker on UK soil at the moment and has a glistening CV from his 20 years at Duval-Leroy, where he revolutionised production with an organic and biodynamic process, and more recently at Leclerc Briant.

30% of annual production is being set aside as reserve wines every year, which is a huge investment for the winery. This outlay will bear fruit in full over the next few years, as the Hambledon wines will just get better and better. I'm fizzed on the future of Hambledon; it will be exciting to see the company realise its own quality potential.

Hambledon Classic Cuvée is an assemblage from the 2014 harvest blended with reserve wines from 2010; a blend of 40% chardonnay, 31% pinot meunier and 29% pinot noir, this fizz sings with identity and grace. Watch out England, and Champagne: this is a step above the competition on both sides of the Channel.

Type: English sparkling, brut
Style: Proper good fizz
Price: ££
Stockists: Specialist
Toast:
Food: Sour-cream Pringles
Occasion: Scotland winning the Calcutta Cup
Website: www.harrowandhope.com

Tasting note: *Nose is super-appealing: pinot noir dominates with red apple, soft bruised plum fruit, and toast and scone notes. Typically English mind you, with some orchard and hedgerow tones. Full palate, creamy and rich with soft foaming mousse. Fruity and apparent, a little sweet but there is saline and purity there. Toastiness, which will develop.*

74 *

HARROW & HOPE BRUT RESERVE

WINEMAKER HENRY LAITHWAITE WAS BORN WITH WINE IN HIS BLOOD, son of legendary Tony Laithwaite, who knows a thing or two about great wine! Hope & Harrow is a true family affair, run and owned by Henry and wife Kaye, with help from their gorgeous French Labrador Alfie.

The vineyard is situated in the Chiltern Hills above the Thames valley, and the flinty soils play absolute havoc, piercing tractor tyres and wellington boots alike, but flavour the production of brilliant sparkling wine. Henry was a winemaker in Australia and Bordeaux before he started on this project, and you can feel and taste it in his wines. He cleverly used oak barrels (second-hand chardonnay barrels from the Laithwaites' winery in Castillion – family perks) for his reserve wine which gives much more complexity, spice and weight to the finished wines. He has a huge amount of care and respect for his grape varieties and captures the varietal character of chardonnay and pinot noir masterfully, with a guiding hand from Tony Jordan (of Moët & Chandon).

Henry's Brut Reserve is a blend of the three champagne grapes grown in the vineyard's flinty soils next to the winery. Henry is big fan of Bollinger and Charles Heidsieck (also two of my favourite champagne brands) and you can taste it in his oxidative styles. Unlike many English sparkling producers, H&H hasn't rushed its wines to market, which can be a huge detriment to quality but better for cash flow. Instead it releases only when the wines are ready. For me, these are some of the richest and most 'champagne like' English sparklings available, remarkable quality considering how young the vines are. Bravo Henry, Kaye and Alfie. H&H has a very bright future.

Type: English sparking, brut, vintage
Style: A flawless foamer
Price: ££££
Stockists: Specialist
Toast: 🍞🍞🍞
Food: Arbroath smokies
Occasion: Finished your first 100 mile cycle
Website: www.hattingleyvalley.co.uk

Tasting note: *Apple crumble with vanilla custard, pricked by the sharp twang of lemon sherbet. Spices, and foaming golden weight, propel the KC to lofty heights of English quality. The oak is seasoning, adding weight and sweet notes, clear acid profile and lovely salinity. Topper.*

75 *

HATTINGLEY VALLEY KINGS CUVÉE 2013

SIMON ROBINSON PLANTED A 28-ACRE SOUTH-FACING SITE IN THE rolling hills of Hampshire in 2008. Owners Simon and Nicola now manage 60 acres including sites in east Hampshire. They also crush grapes from other wineries, making them the largest contract winemakers in England and helping them cover the vast costs of setting up a winery from scratch.

Hampshire is home to some of the best-situated vines in the UK because of the climate and chalk soils, identical to those in Champagne. Hattingley Valley first launched its carefully made and precise wines in 2013, and ever since it has been building a reputation as a serious player in the UK wine industry. The winery prides itself on the clever use of oak for primary fermentation and its reserve wines, which builds complexity and weight on the palate, otherwise difficult to gain from young vines.

The very limited release of Kings Cuvée is a dream; it's the company's top expression with a price tag to match, a blend of the best parcels of chardonnay and pinot noir, fermented then aged in old oak barrels for eight months, prior to secondary fermentation in bottle. There is no other wine like it in the UK. After scrutinising tasting, only the best barrels are selected for the Kings Cuvée; just 7 out of 180! The selection and attention to detail is commendable: the wine is bottled ready for secondary fermentation, where it stays on lees for 30 months, gaining further weight, complexity and toasty richness. Dosed at under 4 grams of sugar a bottle, this is a discerning style of English sparkling, and will benefit from further cellaring. Considering how young the winery is, Hattingley Valley has a bright future; it is making great wines now, and will only improve.

Type: England sparkling rosé, vintage
Style: Lady of the manor in fishnets
Price: £££
Stockists: Specialist
Toast:
Food: Grilled prawns, shell-on, with fresh tomato and chilli
Occasion: Winter barbeque
Website: https://hoffmannandrathbonestore.co.uk

Tasting note: Gleaming pink with a salmon edge; the nose is super-appealing with raspberry ice cream, tuck-shop bootlaces and pink grapefruit, strawberries too with a mix of crunchy and stewed. The palate is a pleasure, creamy; think strawberry ice cream in a Walls cone! Sweet fruit, fresh and biscuity with oatmeal and some savoury garden herbs. There is a saline edge and the acid is high, but the sweetness of fruit is lubricating. Foaming fizz, topper.

76*

HOFFMANN & RATHBONE ROSÉ RÉSERVE 2011

HUSBAND AND WIFE TEAM ULRICH HOFFMANN AND BIRGIT RATHBONE run this stylish estate in the south-east of England. Ulrich has made wine in many places around the world, including nearby stints at Bolney and Gusbourne estates in England. Now he has settled his skillset to the creation of his own breed of super-serious and seductive sparklings in Sussex.

Their range is not large, but the attention to detail and quality is impressive, and there is a thorough endeavour to build quality into their wines at every step, which you can taste in every sip. Also got to say, perhaps polarising, I think their labels are packaging bangin, far removed from a lot of the standardised labels you see on the shelves.

The Rosé Réserve is a masterpiece, created by using grapes from four different vineyards of the estate with five separate pinot noir components, including a late-harvest pinot which is vinified as a red wine and blended in to create the rosé. Many of the best champagne rosés are made this way but it is fairly unusual for the UK. It gives more depth and savouriness to the finished style. The pinot-based blend is backed up with 15% barrel-fermented chardonnay, which gives it electric backbone of spicy freshness.

This is a clever wine, agile and elegant, turbo-charged by 40 months on lees (15 months is a minimum in Champagne), lending more weight to the palate and toasted notes. Bravo to Ulrich: this rosé gives most pink champagnes a run for their money.

Type: Canadian sparkling icewine
Style: The nectar of the gods
Price: £££
Stockists: Specialist
Toast: 0
Food: Sticky toffee pudding or punchy cheeses
Occasion: Your brother's 18th
Website: www.inniskillin.com

Tasting note: *This wine boggles both mind and taste sensations. Golden peaches and guavas smothered in honey fill the nose. The palate is all Opal Fruits, dried apricots, lychees and pineapple, super-sweet yet utterly fresh, balanced by a gentle, foaming sparkle and an icy acidity which cleanses the palate with a torrential wash of glacial refreshment.*

77*

INNISKILLIN NIAGARA SPARKLING VIDAL ICEWINE

Icewine is originally from the cold-climate regions of Europe but few live up to the quality of Canadian Inniskillin. The company was founded in 1975 by Karl Kaiser and Donald Ziraldo, who believed in the quality potential for fine wine on the Niagara Peninsula. The climate is only just suitable for grape ripening, and this marginal climate means it is perfect for the production of icewine. They first produced icewine, made from Vidal grapes from selected vineyards on the Niagara lake, in the severe winter of 1984. On its release, it put Canadian viticulture and the Niagara Peninsula on the fine wine map forever.

Most wines in the northern hemisphere are harvested between August and October. For Inniskillin, the grapes reach full ripeness in October, but are left untouched on the vines until the first deep freeze of winter; the grapes raisin on the vines, dehydrating, gaining concentration of flavours, aromas, acids and sugars.

The grapes are picked under a full moon, when the temperatures drop to –10°C and the grapes are frozen solid. When pressed the water is removed as ice, and the concentrated golden nectar is kept. Yields for icewine are only 10% of a normal bottle, but carrying 100% of the flavour, which translates into lip-puckering intensity in the finished wine. Fermentation takes place slowly due to the high residual sugar, so the wine only reaches 9.5% alcohol while the sweetness is almost 300g/litre (cola cola is 100 g/litre). The bubbles are captured by the tank method, trapping the CO_2 and dissolving it back into the rich, golden sweetness. This truly is a unique wine, one of the only examples in the world, and drinking it is one of life's great pleasures.

Type: Pink moscato
Style: An Aussie Turkish delight
Price: £
Stockists: High street
Toast: 0
Food: Strawberry ice cream
Occasion: Hair of the dog
Website: www.innocentbystander.com.au

Tasting note: *Candy floss, blackcurrants, strawberry bootlaces and sugared Turkish delight. Intensely sweet, fizzy and grapey: blood oranges, bottled fun.*

78 *

INNOCENT BYSTANDER MOSCATO 2017

INNOCENT BYSTANDER HAS MADE A NAME FOR ITSELF OVER RECENT years for exceptional quality and well-priced wines from Victoria, Australia. Although the winemakers are more famous for their chardonnay and pinot noir, both readily available in the UK, it's the recent success of their pink moscato which sparked my attention.

They introduced small amounts of it in 2006 and now sell it domestically by the bucket load. It didn't make a splash over here until longstanding Innocent Bystander fan Jamie Oliver ordered a stack of it for his restaurants, then they knew they were on to a winner! The style of their moscato has a nod to original Italian styles: light, fruity and fizzy, but with a fun-loving Aussie twist.

It is harvested at the dead of night, to keep the grapes nice and cool. They use two grapes: the classic moscato of Alexandria, which is one of the few grapes in the world to actually taste of grapes, and black muscat, which adds more depth of fruit and twang on the palate. The vivid colour is all natural, obtained from 6 hours of skin contact, and the fizz is captured by the charmat method. It's impossible not to enjoy this wine, and at a light 5.5% alcohol it can be drunk any time of day! I don't openly condone drink at breakfast, unless totally necessary, but this would be ideal with a bowl of Lucky Charms.

Type: Tasmanian, brut
Style: Devilishly delicious fizz
Price: ££
Stockists: High street
Toast:
Food: Grilled shrimp obviously
Occasion: Beach BBQ
Website: www.jansz.com.au

Tasting note: *Floral hits, citrus fruits, green mango and Greggs. There is a bright berry character on the palate, a touch toasty with roasted nuts and cappuccino foam, spritzed by full fizz, a long finish with ripe lemons and zippy acid, as fresh as an Antarctic current.*

79*

JANSZ TASMANIA PREMIUM CUVÉE

JANSZ IS FIERCELY TASMANIAN; THE NAME PAYS TRIBUTE TO THE DUTCH explorer Abel Janszoon Tasman who first spotted the island in 1642, when Dom Pérignon was four years old. Jansz winery was set up and planted in 1975 in the Piper's River region of the Island, located in the north-east. This little corner of the island has since been coined 'Sparkling Tasmania' by locals for the quality of fizzers out of the area. It's cool-climate viticulture in Tasmania, but the proximity to the Bass Strait and the mediating ocean breezes allow the perfect, slow maturation of grapes, giving powerfully flavoured wine. The soils here are nuts, the vines are planted directly on a bed of pure, red, free-draining basalt giving a distinctly Tasmania signature to the sparkling wines.

In 1986 the Jansz owners were joined by champagne royalty, Louis Roederer, who saw huge quality potential in this cool-climate site for the production of world-class fizzers. The current owners are vignerons Yalumba, who are furthering the quest for quality, and the wines have never been better.

Detailed selection in the vineyards and winery further aid the complexity and utterly delightful drinkability of this Tasi fizzer. Following the *méthode traditionnelle* or *méthode Tasmanoise*, the classic blend of chardonnay and pinot noir is aged on lees for over two years to gain richness and toasty complexity. I'm a big fan of Yalumba and Jansz – no jokes – this is one of the better-value fizzers on our supermarket shelves.

Type: Sparkling sake rice wine, no vintage
Style: Fizzy Samurai freshness
Price: ££
Stockists: Specialist
Toast: 0
Food: Sushi every day, all the time
Occasion: Opening ceremony of Rugby World Cup
Website: http://akashi-tai.com

Tasting note: *Asian flavours which you don't naturally associate with wine or beverages challenge and inspire; this wee bottle is a sumo wrestler of taste. Lightly sparkling with mineral flavour supported by lemon grass, starch, green tea, steely zest.*

80 *

JUNMAI GINJO SPARKLING SAKE

THE ORIGINS OF FERMENTED RICE WINE PREDATE HISTORY; CHAMPAGNE is a toddler in comparison! Rice wine is made historically in China and Asia, and there are as many different rice wines in the world as there are wines . . . could be my next book. Sake, the Japanese fermented rice wine, has been made for centuries, but it's only fairly recently been readily available in the UK high streets, propelled by our love of Japanese cuisine.

Akashi-Tai brewery (yes, sake is brewed like beer rather than vinified like wine) has been creating sake since 1856, using expertise passed through the family generations. The land around the coastal town of Akashi is ideal for the cultivation of rice, with a lot of natural fresh springs in the region supplying the purest water, vital for quality sake. Sake is made by polishing the rice in steel or ceramic drums, then water is added to achieve a fermentable starch which can then be brewed into alcohol. The Junmai Ginjo is taken one step further and, like the *méthode traditionnelle*, it re-ferments in bottle which creates a naturally sparkling sake.

Sake styles come in many different forms and flavours, and can offer a brilliant alternative to your usual drinking habits. Asian cuisine can often fight against the classical flavours and structures of wine, but sake is pure joy with the challenging, umani or spicy flavours of the East.

Type: Cava, brut nature, multi-vintage
Style: Spanish delight
Price: ££
Stockists: High street
Toast:
Food: Mixed tapas obvs
Occasion: Barcelona vs Real Madrid
Website: www.juveycamps.com/en

Tasting note: *Free-run juice of white peaches and lemons flow into wild honey, toast and smoky, flinty flavours. The palate is distinctly fizzy, with bitter almond, stone fruit and gleaming freshness.*

81*

JUVE Y CAMPS RESERVA DE LA FAMILIA GRAN RESERVA

CAVA IS MADE IN EXACTLY THE SAME WAY AS CHAMPAGNE, AND its style (which is different from champagne) can produce exceptional quality and offer brilliant value. One of the top-of-the-pops players, Juve Y Camps, has a winemaking history spanning over 200 years. Since 1921, the company has quickly forged a reputation for making exceptional cava, which is often the choice for the Spanish royalty or for the tapas bars of local Barcelona.

Launched in 1976 and originally destined for family consumption, the Reserva de la Familia is now their best-selling wine. An expression is true to the region's heritage and uses only indigenous grapes of macabeo, parellada and xarel-lo.

The winery owns multiple vineyard areas and the Reserva de la Familia is a mix of top wines from a mixture of their vineyards from Espiells, Can Massana and La Cuscona estates, favouring higher altitudes, older vines and limestone soils for increased minerality and freshness in the wines.

A blend of 55% xarel-lo, 35% macabeo and splash of 10% parellada make up the Gran Reserva; after the base wines are made, each bottle rests in the *cava* or caves for at least 36 months, softening the wine and building toasty complexity. Brut nature, this wine is super-clean and drier than most champagnes, but the extended time on lees means it is soft, foaming and dangerously drinkable. *Salud*!

Type: South African, Cape Classique, vintage
Style: Distinctly African in a French dress
Price: £££
Stockists: Specialist
Toast: 🍞🍞🍞
Food: Illicit crayfish on the *brai*
Occasion: Surviving a surf in shark-infested waters!
Website: www.kleinconstantia.com

Tasting note: *Light and airy on the nose, with aromas of baked bread, wild greens, apples and ripe pears. The palate is foaming with fizz, zesty and mineral from the ancient soils and fresh ocean breezes. Long, pleasing and classical.*

82*

KLEIN CONSTANTIA BRUT 2014

LAST TIME I VISITED SOUTH AFRICA I WENT SURFING IN MUIZENBERG, a few miles down the coast from where this wine is made. The waves were good but it's super-sharky out there, so I was eager to have my feet back on dry land and have a glass of Cape Classique to celebrate. Klein Constantia is one of the oldest estates in South Africa, established by the first Governor of Cape Town in 1685.

Under the Constantiaberg mountain, the winery has ocean influence on two sides, providing a unique and cool climate for establishing world-class viticulture, with epic views down the Constantia valley and out to the swell, and sharks, of False Bay. The farm rises straight up from the ocean, consistently battered by ocean winds, producing an unusually cold micro-climate for this country. In fact it's one of the coldest estates in the Cape, and produces more Old-World styles because of it. The soils are 600-million-year-old decomposed granite, which give identity and minerality to the wines. The clay content provides good water retention, which is increasingly critical for the wines of the Western Cape.

The estate is most famous for Vin de Constance, one of the best sweet wines in the world with over 300 years of history. It was treasured above any other sweet wine in the European courts in the eighteenth and nineteenth centuries. French kings chartered ships just to get it, and Napoleon drank it to find solace during his exile. I prefer the bubbles.

Constantia is perfectly situated to produce quality fizz. Its MCC (Méthode Cap Classique) is one of the best fizzers in South Africa. It is 100% chardonnay, all from a single vineyard on the lower slopes of the mountain. Aged on lees for 33 months before disgorging, this *lekka* MCC rivals many blanc de blancs that cost twice as much.

Type: Sparkling shiraz, vintage
Style: An Aussie institution
Price: £££
Stockists: Specialist
Toast: 🍞🍞
Food: As the winery suggest: bacon and eggs! Steak with red peppercorns would be bangin'
Occasion: Meat feast
Website: www.majellawines.com.au

Tasting note: *The colour is dark ruby, vibrant with purple flashes on foaming intensity. Black fruit, cassis, spiced damson which flow into the palate, rich with cleaning freshness from the fizzy mousse. Luscious and round, with coffee notes, hints of plum, nutmeg, liquorice, and supple, fruit-driven tannins.*

83*

MAJELLA SPARKLING SHIRAZ

THE LYNN FAMILY WHO OWN MAJELLA WERE, AND STILL ARE, SHEEP farmers. They planted a block of shiraz vines back in 1968, but historically sold their grapes to Hardy's or Wynns. Other the years these contracts fell through and the family were left with a load of top-quality shiraz left on the vine. Although the lambs were the top priority at the time, in 1991 the Lynns bit the bullet and started making their own wines at the family farm. A generation down the line, and they have carved a serious reputation for their range of high-quality wines from Coonawara: an area famous for some of the best wines in Australia, based on the distinctive mineral red soils of the region.

I love wines that polarise, and this wine won't be for everyone. It is unusual, but the style has a cult following back in Australia, and also here in the UK. It is the richest, darkest, fullest sparkling wine available in the world, and there are only handful of producers worthy of note, none more so than Majella. Sparkling red wines are a great tradition in Australia, usually drunk on the beach at Christmas.

If you have ever had Aussie shiraz, you will know how fruity and intense it can be, especially when the wine is from a single low-yielding estate with great soils, as in Coonawara. The base wine for Majella Sparkling Shiraz is matured in oak for six months; at that point it could be bottled as a rich shiraz! But it is then left on the lees following secondary fermentation for 24 months. The wine is then disgorged and topped up with a vintage port for extra complexity. The results are big, dark, juicy, spicy shiraz, rich in colour and tannins, toasty flavours and foaming mousse. Once you are over the sheer surprise of this, it is a glorious awakening to a new way to enjoy sparkling, i.e. with steak!

Type: Moscato d'Asti, vintage
Style: The perfect pick-me-up
Price: £
Stockists: High street
Toast: 0
Food: Perfect on its own, but would be mega with panettone bread & butter pudding, or fruit salad
Occasion: You will never regret opening a moscato d'Asti
Website: www.marcarini.it

Tasting note: *Glorious starburst-style sweet fruit and gushing with lip-puckering tangfastic freshness. Apple, mango, pineapple and Tropicana fruit flavours supersoaker you with cream-soda style fizz. Lightly sparking, frothingly delicious and dangerously gluggable.*

84*

MARCARINI MOSCATO D'ASTI

Moscato d'Asti is retro and, like some other cheerful European wines, it came into favour in the 1970s and 1980s, only to fall on its own sweet sword of success. But times are a changing; since 2011, moscato sales have skyrocketed, particularly in the USA. The rise has been because of its price point, its easy-drinking style and bizarrely the adoption of moscato d'Asti as the drink of choice by some of the hip-hop culture. Nicki Minaj even launched her own label, but her fizz didn't make my ruthless taste test I'm afraid.

There is a quality ceiling to moscato, sure: it's cheap, cheerful and sweet. But if you know what you're buying into, then it's one of the best-value wines out there. I bloody love it. Moscato can be made in a host of styles, but the northern Italians arrest the fermentation, capping the alcohol at 5.5% when the wines are only gently sparkling. The left-over sugar gives the wine a delicious grapey sweetness, which can be drunk any time of the day. Historically it was the perfect brunch or lunch wine for vineyard workers, as they could see off a few glasses and still be compos mentis in the afternoon.

Six generations of family winemaking mean the Marcarinis know exactly what they are doing; they bring the same attention to detail and passion to their moscato as they do to their world-class barolo and still wines, Their moscato is a far cry from some of the supermarket styles available; they have smaller yields, focusing the concentration of fruit from vineyards close to 300 metres of altitude, which slows the grapes ripening and increases flavour development. Manuel Marchetti at the winery describes moscato as 'a wine of happiness and friendship', and, honestly, it is almost impossible to taste this wine and not smile.

Type: Prosecco DOCG, brut, vintage
Style: If Carlsburg did prosecco …
Price: ££
Stockists: Specialist
Toast: 0
Food: Soft-shell Venetian crabs
Occasion: First day of the holidays
Website: www.masottina.it

Tasting note: *Water-white, green flashes. The nose is semi-aromatic and lightly floral with some white blossom notes, altogether quite tightly wound with cool steel and green apple zap, lightly floral. More* terroir *driven. Clean and mineral, sour apple and ripe pear meet for a lovely balance of ripeness and freshness. The palate is a wash of acid and salinity, with a pleasing touch of sweet apple. Complex to a degree if it wasn't so damn drinkable.*

85*

MASOTTINA PROSECCO LE RIVE DI OGLIANO

I'M NOT SURE WHICH IS MORE OF A MOUTHFUL: THE BRILLIANCE OF fruit, minerality and fizz of this single-vineyard prosecco or its full name, Le Rive di Ogliano Extra Dry Conegliano Valdobbiadene Prosecco Superiore DOCG, which is why the Masottina brothers are renaming their top expression of the estate 'RDO' from the 2017 vintage. A nod to Bollinger's Recently Discouraged series perhaps.

This is one of the best proseccos out there, single-vineyard from 40–60-year-old glera vines in a UNESCO-certified Area of Natural Beauty in rolling hills between the towns of Conegliano and Valdobbiadene. Not only are these the most beautiful vineyards in the area with the alpine backdrop and patchwork hills of vines, they are also the most prized and historical prosecco vineyards in the region.

The vineyards here are higher in altitude and cooler, due to their exposure to the chilly Alpine winds to the north, which slows the ripening and increases complexity in the grapes, aided by the ancient glacial soils and chalky soils (chalk is king for sparkling wines). The old vines also have a major impact, as the yield is much lower than younger more vigorous vines and produces fruit of more flavour and complexity.

Sweeter than the brut, at extra dry the Rive di Ogliano has 12 grams of sugar per bottle, so over 1 gram of sweetness in every glass, which softens the backbone of minerality and eases drinkability! The fermentations are among the longest for prosecco, taking five months in total, which again aids complexity and flavour. The Masottina signature is clean and harmonious wines: this is a true example of the family's brilliant winemaking.

Type: Prosecco DOC, brut
Style: Bobbing for apples in an alpine stream
Price: £
Stockists: High street
Toast: 0
Food: Salt and vinegar crisps, and dip
Occasion: Friday afternoon
Website: www.masottina.it

Tasting note: *Water-white, foaming with green-apple flashes. The nose is a smack of pear drops, crunchy apple skin, white flowers and a touch of stinging nettle, backed up by some ripe apricot and white peach. Super-clean and semi-aromatic. The palate is a wash of cool alpine acidity, touch of Appletise sweetness, pear and green mango, more floral notes and with mineral zip. The fizz is lively but foaming, mellowed by a touch of a sugar rush at the end. WARNING: this is dangerously moreish, not to drink with in-laws or esteemed work colleagues.*

86*

MASOTTINA PROSECCO TREVISO BRUT

THE MASOTTINA FAMILY BEGAN MAKING WINE IN 1946, STARTING with 4 hectares of vines around the town of Conegliano in the rolling glacial foothills of the Italian Alps. Today this family owns 100 hectares of primetime vineyards, and are still expanding.

Masottina make their wines in a cooler region than most of the Prosecco area; it is higher altitude, and the alpine winds are channelled directly over the precious glera vines. The grapes grow slowly, ripen later and have more concentration and flavour than those of the vineyards in the open plains to the south (where most prosecco is produced). The Masottina winery is state of the art and squeaky clean, as are the wines, which are meticulously controlled and beautifully elegant.

The Treviso Brut is their best-selling estate prosecco; labelled brut it has just over 8 grams of sugar per bottle, so on the drier end of the prosecco sweetness scale. This means it is a purer, cleaner style of the famous foaming wine and more refreshing than average supermarket examples. What really sets this prosecco apart from the raff is the fermentation, which for prosecco can often be a quick and rushed process. Filippo and Francesco Masottina encourage a long, slow fermentation for both the first still wine fermentation and the secondary fermentation (where you capture the bubbles); this boosts complexity of flavour and gives more weight and creaminess on the palate, or *cremoso* as the locals would say. The winery is all gravity fed, and all the top wines are hand harvested and whole-bunch pressed, using only best-quality free-run juice. This attention and care for prosecco is remarkable – if you like your proseccos fruity and fizzy you can't find better quality.

Type: Chilean sparkling rosé, brut, multi-vintage
Style: Blushing over the Andes
Price: ££
Stockists: High street
Toast:
Food: Tuna ceviche
Occasion: Just saved £100 on your car insurance
Website: www.migueltorres.cl

Tasting note: *Bright pink, crunchy and frothy with wild strawberries, savoury edges and cassis leaf on the nose. The palate is clean and cherry-fruity, and as fresh as an Andean breeze up your poncho.*

87*

MIGUEL TORRES CHILE ESTELADO ROSÉ

CHILE IS AN AMAZING COUNTRY, WINE ASIDE. IT IS 2,670 MILES long, the most volcanic place on earth and weaves from rolling vineyards, volcano, jungle, desert, to scale-defying Andean mountains, rugged and pristine coastlines, buzzing cosmopolitan cites and more. The diversity of climate and landscape is matched only by the diversity of cultures and wine styles. I love the wines of Chile and it's a shame more fine Chilean examples don't make it to our shelves. Chile has the largest average winery size in the world. This tells us it is dominated by big, commercial wineries. But some of the larger names, like Miguel Torres, use their influence for the good of the grapes and the people.

In 2007 a project was undertaken between the Ministry of Agriculture, University of Talca and Miguel Torres Chile to research ways of producing delicious and sustainable wines from Chile's most historical grape: pais. Introduced by Spanish settlers over 500 years ago, it is now the second most planted grape in Chile. But demand has slumped over the years in favour of international grapes like merlot and cabernet. This means hundreds of families over thousands of acres of land have fallen on uncertain times as the price of their harvest has dropped, causing financial uncertainty.

As a result of this project, Miguel Torres created the world's first sparkling pais, Estelado Rosé, and the results are tremendous. The grape, traditionally used for cheap bulk wine for domestic consumption, has a pure, crunchy cherry-style flavour with naturally high acid and is perfect for sparkling wine. Long forgotten and undervalued, this grape is now enjoying a frothy surge of popularity 500 years after being introduced.

Type: Lambrusco, vintage
Style: Adult Vimto
Price: ££
Stockists: Specialist
Toast:
Food: Pizza, pasta, pizza, pasta, pizza, BBQ
Occasion: You could die tomorrow – have a bloomin' glass!
Website: https://montedellevigne.it/en

Tasting note: *Foaming and dark in colour with black cherry and purple flashes. So juicy! Foaming out the glass with damson, plum, cassis and forest fruits. The palate is dry with creamy dark fruit and intensity, almost raspberry-ripple ice cream, but with a lick of green tannins and Italian mixed spices – amazing. Tannins are evident, as is the acidity: the hallmark of great Italian wines.*

88*

MONTE DELLE VIGNE LAMBRUSCO 2016

MONTE DELLE VIGNE IS ONE OF THE MODERN WAVE OF WINE producers in Emilia-Romagna reinventing the traditional styles of the region. You can ask many people about lambrusco and most will tell you it's cheap, sweet and fizzy. Defining identity is a challenge for producers, as lambrusco comes from a large area and is made in many different styles: sweet, fizzy, dry, white, rosato, red, . . . who knows what it tastes like?

Now, believe me, because I have been pushing for a lambrusco comeback for years. It is one of the great wines of Italy, not because it's expensive, age worthy or famous, but because it is bloody brilliant to drink. Emilia-Romagna has some of the best cuisine in Italy, which includes tortellini, balsamico, prosciutto, and the best cheese there is, Parmigiano Reggiano. Do you think the generations of locals were drinking bad wine when they created the world's most famous and sought-after foods? NO! They were drinking lambrusco, but it has a popularity issue overseas. I'm on a mission to change this.

This will challenge some drinkers. It's different: a dark, tannic, fizzy fruit bomb, it is all encompassing, having the best attributes of red wine (tannin, flavour and colour) but still fresh and fizzy.

Made exclusively from local lambrusco maestri grape, this fruity wee number starts life as a red wine, being macerated on the skins for 25 days, gaining colour, fruity flavour and tannin. It is then made like a prosecco, retaining the sparkling in tank and dissolving it back into the wine. The results are delicious. I literally can't get enough of it and can't fathom why it isn't more popular. Bring on the revolution!

Type: English sparkling, brut, vintage
Style: Bridging
Price: ££££
Stockists: Specialist
Toast:
Food: Line-caught mackerel
Occasion: Slipping into your honeymoon
Website: http://nyetimber.com

Tasting note: *McIntosh Red apples cut up on freshly baked muffins, with delicate floral notes and citrus peel, express themselves on the nose. The palate is a gushing waterfall of fresh lemon, grapefruit and delish hobnob character with a fine, and cleverly woven, mousse. Cracking wine with excellent minerality, a fine expression indeed.*

89★

NYETIMBER TILLINGTON 2013

NYETIMBER IS THE BEST-KNOWN ENGLISH SPARKLING WINE, AND consistently the most delicious. The Nyetimber farmstead had a first mention in 1086 in the Doomsday Book; 900 years later, two Americans Sandy and Stuart Moss were among the first to plant champagne grapes on their West Sussex and Hampshire chalk-ridden soils, in 1988.

They quickly forged a reputation as the best English sparkling wine producer, with an attitude to selling like a Grande Marque champagne: smart advertising and key sponsorship deals paired with great packaging and brilliant quality. They have been surprising and delighting drinkers ever since its launch. Nyetimber was the first English wine to beat a champagne in a blind tasting, and ever since it has been a benchmark of quality in the UK.

Nyetimber has been pushing the envelope of quality since the beginning, but never more so than since winemaker Cherie Spriggs has been in charge. She has quickly risen to be one of the most respected *chefs de cave*s in the UK, and the first woman ever to win sparkling winemaker of the year at the wine world Oscars.

This special wine was identified by Cherie in 2009 when she noticed that the Tillington Vineyard produced exceptional pinot noir. So good that they separated it and launched with the 09 vintage. The 2013 is their third release, and the quality is only improving with the increasing vine maturity. A blend of 76% pinot noir and 24% chardonnay, the Tillington has been rested on lees for over three years under the watchful eye of Cherie. Only a few thousand bottles are made from this special vineyard, and each bottle is individually numbered. This fizzer is ready to be drunk now, with its crystalline freshness and fruity nature.

Type: Prosecco DOCG, brut
Style: Mineral intelligence
Price: ££
Stockists: Specialist
Toast:
Food: Sashimi or sushi
Occasion: First dinner in your new home, even if it's a
Pot Noodle
Website: https://cartizzepdc.com/en

Tasting note: *This is a pure expression of the Cartizze land, sun-filled views and chilly alpine winds with flavours of ripe pear, apple, white blossom and gorse flowers. The palate is as fresh as a glacial torrent, drier than most proseccos you will have ever tasted with a compelling savoury edge. Direct on the palate rather than sweet, with rock-hopping mineral notes.*

90*

PDC PROSECCO VALDOBBIADENE SUPERIORE DI CARTIZZE BRUT

PDC IS THE BRAINCHILD OF PIETRO DE CONTI, AND HIS YOUTHFUL and modern outlook to quality of wine, sustainability of viticulture and branding is a breath of fresh air in the prosecco market, which is dominated by commercial brands. Production is limited to 10,000 bottles per year; to put this in context, I have visited prosecco producers who can make 30,000 bottles an hour.

The prosecco vineyard area has expanded rapidly in the last 10 years; this huge growth in a short time has created some confusion for customers, as unknown to many there are different quality expressions for prosecco. The top of the prosecco pops is the Prosecco Superiore from Cartizze DOCG. Located just outside the town of Valdobbiadene, Cartizze represents less than 0.25% of total prosecco production. The delimited area has a perfect combination of cooler climate, altitude, the mineral soils and sun exposure.

The organic viticulture provides vines with a natural environment to produce healthy flavoursome grapes, allowing the roots to dig deep into the mineral clay soils. The vines have an average age of 60, with some as old as 160! These give unique character to the finished wine. All the vines are tended by hand, but the centurion plants need special care and attention: think Mr Miyagi and his bonsai trees. Pietro's vinification is also longer, cooler and more controlled than many other producers; fermentation can take up to 120 days (10 times longer than many other proseccos), allowing more complexity of flavour to develop. These are the purest, driest and best-quality proseccos I have ever come across. Pound for pound I'd rather drink this than many champagnes.

Type: Metodo classico, brut
Style: Fizzing with volcanicity
Price: £££
Stockists: Specialist
Toast: 🍞🍞
Food: Chicken stew with tarragon and leeks, or sushi
Occasion: New Year, new you
Website: https://planeta.it

Tasting note: *Smooth and soft on approach with delicate floral notes, waxy lemons and tantalising passion fruit. Bay leaf and white peach flow over cannoli with pistachios, green and creamy. Wild Mediterranean spices and herbs explode with mineral, earthy energy.*

91*

PLANETA METODO CLASSICO ETNA BRUT

ETNA! IT'S EASY TO UNDERSTAND THE POWER OF THE MOUNTAIN WHEN you are driving in its direction: the open plains of Sicily might be baking at temperatures of 35°C or higher, but Etna, at over 3,000m altitude, is snow-capped all year round – often billowing with smoke, ash and occasionally red hot magma. The magic of the mountain gives black-rock volcanic soils, altitude above the heat of Sicily and the best porcini mushrooms I have ever tasted.

There is a huge buzz about Etna right now as the last fine-wine frontier of Europe. Many famous producers from France and the north of Italy are scaling the volcanic hillside in search of vineyards.

Planeta have more to do with putting Sicily on the worldwide wine map than any other producer. The original family and vineyards are closer to the west coast of Sicily, around the picturesque Lago Arancio (Orange-tree Lake) where they produce the Island's most famous wines. But after their success they have expanded vineyard holdings, most recently up in the hill lands of Etna.

The Planeta fizz is 100% carricante, the original white grape of the mountain. It is grown at close to 1,000m altitude, which slows ripening down and retains the vital acidity needed for high-quality sparkling wine. The carricante grape is very well adapted to sparkling wine production using *metodo classico*. The soils are sand and black rock, which give salinity and volcanicity to the finished wines. Mineral and driven in style, benefiting from 20 months on lees, this wine is a taste of a volcano, on toast.

Type: English sparkling, brut
Style: So fresh and so clean, clean
Price: £££
Stockists: High street
Toast:
Food: Razor clams and lemon
Occasion: Your horse comes through 100/1 at the Plumpton Race Course
Website: www.plumpton.ac.uk

Tasting note: *This is a fresh and clean style of sparkling, showing balanced and fruity flavours of plum and green apple, English hedgerow and lemony fruit.*

92 *

PLUMPTON ESTATE BRUT CLASSIC NV

OPENED IN 1926, PLUMPTON COLLEGE IS AN AGRICULTURAL college based on the chalky South Downs National Park in the rolling East Sussex hills. You can study everything from pig husbandry and veterinary science to viticulture there; I graduated with a Wine Business Degree from there in 2010. The course has changed a lot since I left, but the wider alumni from Plumpton are permeating the global wine industry and many are winemakers around the world – France, South Africa, New Zealand and, of course, England.

Plumpton had a dilemma when I studied there; it was a non-profit university which made better wine than many commercial English wineries. Competing with the market, it wanted to grow for the benefit of its students. Now the English wine market has expanded and there is enough space for everyone to sell their wine, if it's good enough. The newly branded Plumpton Estate Brut Classic is topper; previously known as 'The Dean', it has won multiple awards over the years and is made from vines tended by the eager students. I have a confession: during harvest I was generally too hungover to pick the grapes, to the bubbling annoyance of my lecturers. But luckily for Plumpton there were enough keen beans to pick the grapes, from 10 hectares of vineyards on some of the prime chalky vineyards in England.

Made by students, overseen by winemakers and lecturers Sarah Midgley and Tony Milanowski, the Estate Brut is a classic champagne-type blend of chardonnay, pinot meunier and pinot noir, based on the bumper 2014 vintage, it has spent almost four years on lees gaining wonderful toasty flavours. The hallmark English acid means that this bottle is set to delight now, or will benefit from a couple of years' maturation.

Type: Californian sparkling, brut, multi-vintage
Style: Golden generosity
Price: ££
Stockists: High street
Toast:
Food: Fat stack (pancakes) with buttermilk and strawberries
Occasion: Super Bowl
Website: www.roedererestate.com

Tasting note: *The Quartet Brut is golden and juicy, with orchard fruit, apple pie, toasted hazelnuts and lemony ice cream character. Foaming and smooth on the palate, there are no hard edges, just freshness, fizz and beautiful depth of flavour. Dreamy.*

93*

QUARTET BRUT ANDERSON VALLEY

My first introduction to this dreamboat sparkler was when I was working in a wine shop in Edinburgh, aged 18. Back then I remember it being stunning value, and more delicious than many champagnes we sold. My tastes have changed a little since then, but the quality and value of Quartet haven't; this wine is impressive.

The Californian arm of Champagne Louis Roederer, Quartet builds on centuries of champagne making expertise in the New World. The Anderson Valley lies to the north of San Francisco, a cool haven from the heat of the Golden State. Its proximity to the ocean lends itself to the Roederer style, where a balance of fruity flavours, sugars and acidity is paramount. The founder Jean-Claude Rouzaud is former president of Louis Roederer and sixth generation descendant of the man himself (the original Louis). Quartet, named after the four distinct vineyard sites on the estate, was launched in 1988, and ever since has been included in wine critics' top 100 sparklers in the world (including mine!).

The winemaking follows the *méthode traditionnelle* of course, adapted to suit the warmer climate of California. The blend is a classic champagne split: 60% chardonnay, 40% pinot noir. Reserve wines play a leading role, from a selection of older vintages, some of which have been aged in oak, giving depth of flavour and body to the finished fizzer. With a minimum of two years on lees, Quartet picks up toasty flavours quicker than most champagnes, which means there's no need for further cellaring after purchase.

A riper style of sparkling, significantly French but with Californian warmth. It's easier to drink than many champagnes, with lower acidity and fuller fruit, which I think is why my 18-year-old self was such a big fan.

Type: German sekt, brut, vintage
Style: A bracing slap of lime
Price: ££
Stockists: Specialist
Toast:
Food: Thai fish cakes
Occasion: Holidays booked
Website: www.von-buhl.de

Tasting note: *Lean, fizzy and clean, this German fizzer is a whistle-stop tour of freshness and energy. With lime, green apples and vivacious mineral snap, this wine is a bracing wake-up when you need a pick-me-up.*

94*

REICHSRAT VON BUHL RIESLING BRUT 2015

THE VON BUHL ESTATE HAS PRODUCED QUALITY WINES SINCE 1849 in the Pfalz wine region. The winery has gone through many changes over the years, none more game-changing than when Mathieu Kauffmann joined the team in 2013. Mathieu was the *chef de cave* at Bollinger for years, a true legend in the trade. This speaks volumes, and gives you an insight into the quality and potential of von Buhl.

Although it's more difficult to find German sparkling wines in the UK, they used to be hugely popular here, especially sekt, hock, Black Tower and Blue Nun. But all took a spiralling dip in popularity, and the UK market has never recovered. That said, as the popularity of German wines has decreased, the quality of wines has got better and better. Every journalist, *somm* or wine professional you meet will sing the praises of German wine and its most famous grape, riesling, which is regarded by the wine trade as the best grape on the planet because of its versatility, and the signature high acidity which keeps the wines fresh and the drinker's palate energised. This high acidity also lends itself to the production of brilliant sparkling wine.

Although riesling is famous for some of the best, long-living wines on the planet, sparkling wines made from it are few and far between. Von Buhl use organic grapes to achieve the best wine possible. The wines spend twelve months on lees, gaining a toasty edge while not diminishing the purity of fruit from the pristine flavours of the riesling. This is a banging fizz which rivals many at its price point but offers something different from the norm, combing the best *chef de cave* craftsmanship and von Buhl's exceptional riesling *terroir*. With Mathieu Kauffmann now at the helm, these wines will only get better and better.

Type: English sparkling wine, blanc de noirs, vintage
Style: Juicy McIntosh apple
Price: £££
Stockists: High street
Toast:
Food: Mackerel pate on chunky oatcakes
Occasion: Fish and chips on Brighton pier
Website: www.ridgeview.co.uk

Tasting note: *Fizzing brilliance, deep, golden and super moreish. Red apple, strawberry leaf, toast and earthy sweetness are set alight by fine, foaming fizz and a toasty, malty edge. The finish is clean as a whistle and deliciously creamy.*

95*

RIDGEVIEW BLANC DE NOIRS 2014

THE ROBERTS FAMILY IS LEGENDARY IN THE UK WINE INDUSTRY. Mike Roberts founded Ridgeview Estate on the South Downs of England in 1995 with the aim of creating world-class sparkling wines. He chose the site because the soil is the same mix of chalk and clay found in the Champagne region. The Roberts family are still producing world-class fizz which rivals any produced in England, and many similar styles across the Channel.

Mike's daughter, CEO Tamara, and brother wine-maker Simon have a long list of accolades; they even won the 'Best Sparkling in the World' a few years ago, beating all the top names of champagne for the trophy – c'mon England! They export around the world and have many high-calibre customers including the White House and No.10. Even ol' Queenie is known to be a fan.

The recent rebranding looks the dog's bollocks, which no doubt will propel Ridgeview on to even greater success. Only ever made in the best years; their 2014 limited release Blanc de Noirs is one of the leading examples in the UK, made exclusively from their best vineyards of pinot noir and pinot meunier.

You will notice 'Merret' written on every bottle of Ridgeview on either the capsule or the label. This is an important nod to Christopher Merret, an Englishman who was the first to understand the science behind secondary fermentation in bottle (sparkling wine production) – even before the French! This godfather of English wine doesn't get enough recognition, so bravo to the Roberts family for the shout out.

Type: Prosecco DOCG, extra dry
Style: Fruit salad on a trampoline
Price: £
Stockists: Specialist
Toast: 0
Food: Good conversation
Occasion: Snowday
Website: www.sacchettovini.it

Tasting note: *Alpine apples and pears, ripe on the nose with white flowers and a shot of lime cordial. The foam is a little spikey but its creamy mouthfeel is a flow of seamless, foaming apple, yellow plum and green mango with flashes of bay leaf. Sweeter finish, very moreish.*

96*

SACCHETTO COL DE L'UTIA

PAOLO SACCHETTO AND HIS FAMILY HAVE BEEN MAKING PROSECCO for generations in their home in Trebaseleghe, 25km north of Venice. Paolo's father Filiberto gave his name to their best-selling prosecco 'Fili', which sells in the UK, Germany and USA, but it is their more recent project which really sparked my interest. Paolo is a super-keen skier; I think he wanted a winery closer to the ski-lifts and his new venture is in the hills towards the Dolomites (and the pistes) in the core of the DOCG area. Their single-vineyard *millesimato* or 'vintage' is one of the finest examples in the region.

High up on the steep hills of Tarzo in the heart of the Valdobbiadene, you have incredible views south over the open plains of Prosecco towards the Adriatic and Venice lagoon. In the summer these hills are wild, the forest broken only by a few prime situated vineyards, lush and green. The winters can be very severe; you definitely need a 4 x 4 to access the brand new winery which is perched on the steep slopes of the Col de l'Utia.

Colder nights, more luminosity, longer growing season and the chilly alpine winds all contribute to the extra quality of this single-vineyard expression. Paolo is meticulous in his selection of grapes for his special single-vineyard expression, meaning only the best is good enough.

Long tank fermentation further aids the creaminess and complexity of his top prosecco, sweetened to extra dry at around 9 grams of sugar per litre to give more forgiving fruity character. It also looks the part with its beautiful detailed label.

Type: Long Island sparkling, brut, vintage
Style: Big apple in a glass elevator
Price: £££
Stockists: Very specialist
Toast:
Food: Clam chowder or hot dogs with American mustard
Occasion: Big city living
Website: www.sparklingpointe.com

Tasting note: *Light golden colour, lively and expressive with fresh lemon rind, Babycham with a touch of baked pretzel. On the palate there is a generous creamy mousse, citrus, red apples and touch of toast on the flinty finish.*

97*

SPARKLING POINTE BRUT 2015

YOU WOULD NEVER BELIEVE YOU ARE A FEW HOURS' DRIVE FROM Manhattan when you visit the idyllic splendour of North Fork on Long Island. The winters can be harsh, it's breezy on the coast but the summers are lush, and die-hard champagne lovers Tom and Cynthia Rosicki knew this area showed great potential for quality sparkling wine.

Atlantic gusts run through the 40 acres of vineyard planted on glacial soils with the three classic champagne grapes: chardonnay, pinot noir and pinot meunier. Each cuvée is an authentic taste of Long Island and the personality of the winemaker, Gilles Martin.

Born on the edge of the Champagne region, Gilles obtained a Masters in Oenology from the University of Montpellier, where countless winemakers have cut their teeth. He has worked all over the world, but importantly was the assistant winemaker at the Roederer family estate in California, known to produce some of the best sparkling wines in the New World, and from here Gilles' love and understanding of bubbles was nurtured.

The 2015 Brut is a classic blend of 56% chardonnay, 24% pinot noir, 20% pinot meunier with a low dose of under 4 grams of sugar per bottle, which plays in lovely balance to the naturally high acidity. Eighteen months on lees mean this is not the toastiest of fizzers, but it shows purity and plumpness of fruit and is a true pleasure to knock down the hatch. These wines are difficult to find as most of the production is either sold directly at the cellar, or hoovered up in the city. Amazing to have a NY postcode on a bottle of wine of this quality.

Type: Prosecco DOCG, spumante, extra dry
Style: *La prosecco vita*
Price: ££
Stockists: High street
Toast: 0
Food: Risotto bianco
Occasion: Finishing work on a Tuesday
Website: www.trevisiolspumanti.it

Tasting note: *Yellow plums, orange blossom and green apples are immediately enjoyable, like sticking your nose into a bag of prosecco sweeties. The palate is creaming with soft folds of inviting fizz, as fresh as an alpine stream, as tangy as a fruit bowl.*

98*

TREVISIOL PROSECCO DI VALDOBBIADENE DOCG

BASED RIGHT IN THE HEART OF THE VINE-LOCKED TOWN OF Valdobbiadene, this winery looks like a regal home. On stepping through the threshold you realise this is only a façade, as the boutique winery squeezes under high arches and through large open rooms. The Trevisiol family live above the winery, sleeping metres from the top of the large bubbling tanks underneath. Prosecco dreams.

The Trevisiol family were among the first prosecco winemakers, starting with Luigi Trevisiol in 1898. Paolo Trevisiol has taken over his grandfather's mantle to make some of the region's best sparkling wines from his 25 hectares of prime Valdobbiadene vineyards. This town is one of the historical areas of Prosecco, producing wines with more character and identity. Paolo capitalises on the region's altitude, which extends the growing season, producing more flavoursome grapes.

Paolo doesn't make entry-level wines, rather he makes discerning styles from his own vines, and the quality shines through in every bubble. His creativity and focus on quality have led to his wines being chosen for many famous private labels for the USA and Germany, not yet available in the UK.

His Prosecco di Valdobbiadene, with its distinctive orange label, is grown between altitudes of 300–400 metres, from calcareous soils in the hilly vineyards surrounding the town. The glera vines are up to 40 years old giving smaller yields of flavoursome grapes, which translate into more appealing and tasty prosecco in your glass. The tank fermentation process is also longer than with many producers, adding further flavour, texture and complexity to this bright and dangerously quaffable fizzer. *Grazie Paolo!*

Type: English sparkling, vintage
Style: Crown jewels
Price: ££
Stockists: Specialist
Toast:
Food: Creamy scones
Occasion: State funeral
Website: www.windsorgreatparkvineyard.com

Tasting note: *The garden of England: floral and hedgerow, elderflower with Bramley apple, smoothed in Ambrosia custard. Rhubarb crumble washes through light citrus flowers, a touch of Hovis and light, cream finish.*

99*

WINDSOR GREAT PARK BRUT 2014

We know the Queen is partial to Pol Roger and Bolly, and I couldn't say if her allocation is getting tighter because of Brexit, but English wine is so good even the royal family had to have a pop. In partnership with England's winemaking elite, Ridgeview and the Laithwaites family, 4 hectares of vines were planted in the grounds of Windsor Castle in 2011. Although the Romans originally introduced vines to the UK, it was Henry II who planted grapes at Windsor Castle the first time around, back in the 1100s. Now, 800 years later, Anne Linder and Barbara Laithwaite are tending to the first royal vineyard in centuries, and it started with the release of the 2014.

Arguably a watershed for England's wine industry, the 2014 vintage shows great quality of fruit paired with bumper yields, and for just the second year of production the vines at Windsor have produced a quality sparkling wine. Although Windsor isn't quite at the lofty heights of some English producers, it shows majestic potential. A blend of all three champagne grapes, chardonnay headlining, backed up by pinot noir and meunier, adds fragrance to this floral and grassy English fizzer. The 2014 is drinking well now, quintessentially English with hedgerow and toasty character; however, it would benefit from some time on cork to gain richness and complexity. If you have a spare bob, it wouldn't be a bad idea to hoover up some Windsor 2014 . . . if the royals haven't poured it all for the state banquets.

Type: England sparkling, brut, multi-vintage
Style: Copella fountain
Price: £££
Stockists: Specialist
Toast:
Food: Smoked haddock and hollandaise
Occasion: You've had the all-clear!
Website: www.wyfoldvineyard.com

Tasting note: *Lemon meringue, toffee apple and English meadow mingle on the surface of the foaming bubbles. Touch of spice, white florals and cox apples dominate the palate with some tasty oatcake character. The finish is long, toasted and saline: very good indeed.*

100*

WYFOLD VINEYARD 2013

STARTED BY BARBARA LAITHWAITE AND CHERRY THOMPSON, WYFOLD was always on a path of success. They planted vines in 2003, and have been clearing up in most wine competitions they have entered since then. I used to work for the Laithwaites so am very familiar with the Wyfold wines, and every time I taste them I am impressed. Never more so than when the buying team conducted a blind tasting of 30 or more English sparkling wines one Christmas, all the big names you would expect including a few dead-ringer champagnes. I kid you not, Wyfold was by far the best-scored wine of the day.

Wyfold is one of the few vineyards to be planted in the Chiltern Hills. It's chilly up there; higher altitude and ideal soils mean the vines for the Wyfold winery will improve with time. Deep gravel over a bed of chalk gives Wyfold wine a defined and mineral character which lifts the palate higher than many other English fizzers. The 2013 vintage was made with the help of the Roberts family at Ridgeview, and the quality is testament to the *terroir* of the Chiltern Hills and the careful, meticulous winemaking.

Chardonnay dominant, which suits the chalky soils of the area, blended with a little pinot noir and meunier, this is a classic champagne blend. Four years on lees give enough time to develop seamless toast and fine, golden mousse. I've tasted Wyfold back to 2007; it does age wonderfully well, if you can hang on to a bottle or two. You won't see Wyfold sold in the market, as it is all hoovered up by Laithwaites' wine customers, Raymond Blanc's Le Manoir and loyal Wyfold fans. If Monsieur Blanc is a fan, it's definitely worth a pop.

Type: Israeli sparkling, brut, vintage
Style: Biblical bubbles
Price: ££
Stockists: Specialist
Toast: 🍞🍞🍞🍞
Food: Bread and squid
Occasion: Your brother's bar mitzvah, or finishing a book
Website: www.golanwines.co.il

Tasting note: *Tarte au citron and gripping zest dominate and impress with green apple, fresh pastry and almond notes. Super-fresh, elegantly creamy and foaming, this is a discerning style of blanc de blancs, complex and utterly drinkable.*

101*

YARDEN BLANC
DE BLANCS 2010

WE DON'T OFTEN CONNECT ISRAEL WITH QUALITY WINE, OR WINE-making at all. But the country's high altitudes, ancient soils and a biblical history with viticulture mean Israeli wines have a place on any wine list, including mine.

The booming trade in trendy Tel Aviv, and growing local demand, mean that few of the best of wines are exported. And the ones that are exported can be expensive. You can say the same thing for good Californian, Swiss and Australian wines.

Bordeaux blends for the reds are very good from Israel, but it was the Yarden Blanc de Blancs which was my introduction to Israeli fizz, and it made a lasting impression on me. Given to me blind by my boss and fellow fizz enthusiast, I thought it was champagne …

Golan Heights Winery, founded in 1983, has done a lot to put Israeli wines on the map. It is located in the town of Katzrin within the region of Galilee. This region is considered the best wine appellation in Israel, in the most northern and coldest area of the country, surrounded by snowcapped mountains. The vines grow deep into the volcanic soils and sit at an altitude of between 400m and a munro-smashing 1,200m, where snow during the winters is frequent.

The 2010 Yarden Blanc de Blancs, like a champagne BdB, is produced exclusively from chardonnay grapes grown in the northern Golan Heights. You can feel the high-altitude freshness across the palate; it's fresher than a lot of champagnes! Made strictly to the *méthode traditionnelle* with secondary fermentation in bottle, this bad boy has spent over five years resting on lees gaining beautiful toasty, marzipan flavours. A unique taste that will surprise and impress.

Glossary

★

A

Ancestral method – see *méthode ancestrale*.

Aperol Spritz – Fill wine glass with ice, 2 parts Prosecco to 1 part Aperol, add a dash of soda and garnish with orange slice.

Appellation (AOC) – a defined area of French wine production with its own rules and regulations.

Assemblage – The blending of base wines or *vins clairs* to create champagne.

Autolysis – The technical term for the toasty, biscuit and creamy flavours which develop in champagne after ageing in bottle. This is due to the enzymatic breakdown of yeast cells following the second fermentation. See *Toast*.

B

Barrique – A barrel historically used for transporting or storing wine, but now used for the maturating and ageing of wine. Fermenting or maturing wine in oak barrels imparts the texture and flavours of spices, vanilla, wood, coffee and sweet oxidative notes.

Biodynamic wine – Wine made and farmed biodynamically: hippy winemaking using ancient farming principles including planting and harvesting with the lunar cycle, often producing the best quality wines. Many producers use biodynamic principles but are not certified.

Blanc de blancs – Champagne made from 100% chardonnay.

Blanc de noirs – Champagne made from 100% black grapes; usually pinot noir or pinot meunier or a combination of the two.

Bouquet – Not flowers! The aroma of wine.

Brut – French term for a dry champagne with a little sweetness. A brut champagne must have less than 9 grams of sugar per bottle and is the most popular style, making up 90% of all champagne production.

Brut nature – or extra brut, or ultra brut. These champagne have no added sugar, meaning they are bone dry and extra fresh.

C

Calcutta Cup – Scotland 25 England 13, on 24 February 2018.

Cava – Spanish *méthode traditionnelle* wine. See *méthode traditionnelle*

Chalk – The main soil component which gives champagne is unique quality.

Chardonnay – White grape that accounts for 30% of all champagne production.

CIVC (Comité Interprofessionnel du Vin de Champagne) – The organisation which represents, rules and regulates champagne.

Clos – French for single walled vineyard.

CO_2 – Carbon dioxide gas, which gives wine its bubbles.

Côte des Blancs – Area of Champagne located south of Epernay. It has some of the finest vineyards in the whole region and is famous for the production of chardonnay due to its high chalk content.

Coupe – Boob-shaped glass.

Crayères – Chalk cellars, typically used for ageing and maturing champagne. Some of these incredible cellars were originally built by the Romans and are still in use today.

Crémant – A French sparkling wine, often made using the same technique and same grapes as champagne production but outside the Champagne region.

Cru – Designation of a village where champagne is produced; there are 319 registered villages (or crus) in Champagne.

Cuvée – Cuvée is a blend which makes a specific type of champagne, but is not limited to any particular champagne style. Often used to name a blend, e.g. Bollinger's Special Cuvée.

Cuvée de Prestige – A house's most prestigious and expensive champagne.

D

Demi-sec – Half sweet style of champagne, containing up to 37.5 grams of sugar per bottle.

Disgorgement *(dégorgement)* – The removal of the lees in the neck of the bottle following the remuage or riddling process. This important process was developed by Veuve Clicquot.

Dosage – The 'dose' of sugar added to champagne after disgorgement which will affect the final level of sweetness of a champagne.

Doux – Sweet style of champagne, containing more than 37.5 grams of sugar per bottle.

Durello – High-acid grape from the Veneto region of northeast Italy.

E

Épernay – The capital of Champagne, located directly in the centre of the region, is home to some of the most famous houses: Moët & Chandon, Mercier, Pol Roger, Perrier-Jouët among others. Épernay's Avenue de Champagne is a boulevard of grand proportions, and Champagne's most famous address.

Extra brut – Also known as brut nature or ultra brut, containing less than 4.5 grams of sugar per bottle.

F

Fermentation – The process of yeast eating sugar, turning into alcohol and carbon dioxide.

Flute – A popular sparkling wine glass which looks pretty but impedes the quality of champagne.

Franciacorta – *Méthode traditionnelle* wines based on chardonnay and pinot blanc from Lago d'Iseo in Lombardy in northern Italy.

Frizzante – Light, gently sparkling prosecco often with a flat cork rather than a mushroom.

G

Glera – The name of the grape which is used to make prosecco.

Grand Cru – The designation for the best class of vineyards in Champagne. Out of 319 listed villages in the region only 17 have Grand Cru status.

Grande Marques – The largest and most famous champagne houses, who have strict quality standards. Out of the 300 champagne houses in the region, only 24 are classified as Grande Marque. Grande Marques own vineyards, but often buy in grapes from growers for each vintage.

Grower champagne – A champagne grown, made and bottled by a single producer. Grower champagnes tend to be produced in small quantities, and often don't conform to the commercial styles of a Grand Marque.

H

Hautvillers – The Benedictine Abbey and the spiritual home of champagne, and final resting place of Dom Pérignon.

I

Icewine – Sticky, very sweet wine which has been made from naturally frozen grapes.

L

Lambrusco – frothy sparkling wine from Emilia-Romagna in Italy, produced in various styles from dry and serious to light and sweet. Recommended with a big plate of Parma ham.

Lees (or fine lees) – The deposit of dead yeast cells following fermentation. The time a wine is in contact with lees will impact the toasty flavours of champagne.

M

Malolactic fermentation – A biochemical process which transforms malic acids (green apple) to lactic acids (crème fraiche). There is no right or wrong regarding malo vs. non-malo champagne styles; both will create different styles.

MCC (Méthode Cap Classique) – South African description for the production of *méthode traditionnelle* sparkling wines. See *méthode traditionnelle*.

Millésime – a vintage year of champagne: if a vintage year is given on the label, 100% of the wine must come from that year. Vintage champagne is not an indication of quality, but champagne houses only produce vintage wines in good years, so you can expect a Millésime champagne to be of a high standard.

Méthode ancestrale / Pétillant naturel – The first, original way to make sparkling wine using one fermentation to capture bubbles in the bottle. Now becoming increasingly trendy, favoured by the natural wine movement.

Méthode Champenoise – The correct term for the champagne-making method, also called the traditional method outside the Champagne region. It denotes sparkling wine which has had second fermentation in bottle, correct ageing, riddling and disgorgement.

Minerality – A common wine descriptor which isn't even in the dictionary! It refers to the sapidity and salinity of a wine. In Champagne it translates into flavours of chalk, wet stone and the mineral soils in which the champagne grapes are grown.

Montagne de Reims – Key sub-zone of Champagne, in the hilly district situated between Reims and Épernay. Famous for its chalky soils it produces some of the best wines in the whole region. The dominant grape variety is pinot noir.

Mousse – The fizz of champagne! The mousse is the effervescence of champagne or sparkling wine. The best mousse should have small, foaming and persistent bubbles, exploding with flavour without being aggressively fizzy.

Moscato – Fruity grape which produces light and often sweet sparkling wines, notably from north-west Italy.

N

Natural wine – All wine is natural to a certain extent, but often commercial wines have been tinkered with artificial products during their making. Natural wine and the natural wine movement avoid the use of chemical or further man-made products in wine growing or making; this might include stabilisation or filtration. Natural wine is not a quality definition.

Non-vintage (NV) – The most common of champagnes. NVs are a blend of multiple years of champagne to maintain a consistent style and quality year after year. I prefer to call them multi-vintages champagnes. Most NVs will be released ready to drink, but will benefit from a further six months' cellaring, if you have the patience! NV is not an indication of quality, as NV wine can be produced at many different quality levels.

O

Organic wine – wine made from organically grown grapes. Many producers use organic farming practices but are not certified as organic.

P

Perry – sparkling sweet drink made from pears.

Pétillant naturel – see *Méthode ancestrale*.

Phylloxera – A vine pest, originating in North America, which spread around in the world in the 1800s destroying 99% of vineyards across Europe. It eats the roots of the vines killing them over time. Phylloxera arrived in Champagne in the 1890s and devastated the vineyards. There are still some pre-phylloxera vines in Champagne which are extremely rare and make very expensive champagnes.

Pinot meunier – Often thought of as the lesser of the champagne grapes, which shouldn't be the case. It is Champagne's second most planted red grape, accounting for 32% of all vineyard area and gives yellow plum and fruity flavours to champagne.

Pinot noir – The flagship red grape of champagne, and the most challenging to grow. Pinot noir also produces some of the best and most prized red wine on the planet, famously in nearby Burgundy. Pinot noir accounts for 38% of all Champagne vines.

Press – The apparatus to press the grapes to release the juice from the fruit.

Premier Cru – The second best quality class of all villages in the Champagne region: 42 out of the 319 have Premier Cru status.

Prosecco – Popular fruity sparkling wine from Veneto in north-east Italy.

Punt – The indentation on the bottle of a wine bottle, not an indication of quality!

R

Reductive – A wine which has been made without contact with oxygen; it can display a smoky, sulphurous note, which is a good thing!

Reims – The heart of the Champagne region, and the official capital of the Champagne–Ardenne region. Home of many of the most famous champagne producers including Veuve, Charles Heidsieck and Louis Roederer. Reims has a spectacular cathedral, with the size and splendour of Notre Dame.

Reserve wine – Wine which is kept back in the cellar and used to blend into newer wines to achieve consistency, complexity and quality. Reserve wines can be aged for a long time in steel tank, in oak barrel or in bottle, and this will affect the final taste of the champagne.

Riddling (or remuage) – A process which facilitates the settling of lees into the neck of the champagne bottle so that the sediment can easily be removed by disgorgement.

Riesling – High acid and inspiring white grape originally from Germany, but now grows all over the world.

Rive – Single-vineyard classification for premium prosecco rosé – pink champagne.

S

Sabrage – Opening champagne with a sword (sabre)! This historic method of opening bottles is dangerous and lots of fun.

Sake – Japanese rice wine, sec to medium sweet style, which carries 13–24 grams of sugar per bottle.

Secondary fermentation – What makes champagne champagne! The secondary fermentation in bottle is what creates champagne's fizz and complex, toasty flavours.

Sommelier – Essentially a fancy wine waiter. Traditionally found in fine-dining restaurants, but now *somms* are found in many different areas of the wine industry. A proper *somm* will be trained in restaurants in all aspects of wine, service and cuisine, specialising in food and wine matching.

Spumante – Fully sparkling prosecco.

Sur lees – Literally 'on the lees' referring to how champagne ages in contact with lees following secondary fermentation. See *Lees*.

T

Terroir – No direct English translation: *terroir* is the taste of 'somewhereness', a sensory experience of the place where a wine is made. It can be defined as a complex combination of nature, history, climate and geology to give wine a unique flavour and character of where it is grown.

Tirage – The important step of adding sugar and yeast to the bottle to spark the secondary fermentation in bottle, when you first put wine in bottle following the first fermentation.

Toast – All those lovely toasted, biscuit and creamy flavours which develop in champagne after ageing in bottle. This is due to the enzymatic breakdown of yeast cells following the second fermentation. See *Autolysis*.

Tulip – Especially made wine glass for sparkling and champagne, shaped between a coupe, flute and regular wine glass. An essential purchase for any true fizz fan.

Trento DOC – *Méthode traditionnelle* sparkling wines based on chardonnay and pinot noir from the Trento valley in the Italian alps.

U

Ungrafted vines – Vines planted on original root stocks, before the phylloxera epidemic. These heirloom vines might be planted on sandy or resistant soils and will produce small yields of powerfully flavoured grapes.

V

Vallée de la Marne – An important sub-zone of Champagne where pinot meunier is the dominant grape variety.

Veneto – Wide region of north-east Italy where prosecco is made.

Vieilles vignes – Literally, old vines. Older vines can give wines and champagnes a unique and complex style due to the small quantities of grapes that they produce.

Vin clair – The base *clear wine* of champagne, before it is blended and goes through second fermentation.

Vinification – Winemaking.

Vintage – See *Millésime*.

Viticulture – The science and production of grapes.

W

Wild fermentation – A fermentation using wild or indigenous yeasts, which can be slower and less uniform but can give more interesting flavours.

Y

Yeast – A living single-cell organism. When in proximity with sugar or starch it converts into alcohol and carbon dioxide.

Z

Żyw – pronounced Zhiv! Think Dr Zhivago.

Acknowledgements

★

Firstly, thank you to the wine-growers, the grape pickers, the cellar hands, winemakers and sellers. Without the great wines and sparklers they create and market, the world would be a lot less enjoyable, and this book would certainly not be written.

To my agent, who I have so much more to thank for than time or space allows. Thank you to all at Birlinn for believing in this book, particularly to Neville Moir and Mairi Sutherland, who took my rough prose and metamorphosised the text into the effervescent delight you are reading.

Picture credits: special thanks to Davinder Samrai @ Freight, my friend William Van Esland, and to all the producers who supplied images and samples. Thanks also to those who submitted samples that I didn't include. To my employer, Berry Bros. & Rudd, for all their support, which reaches far above the historic cellars of No.3 St James. To my gorgeous fiancée Yvie for her tireless patience; I do my best to test it. And finally, to all my friends, who selflessly helped me finish bottles after my tasting notes were written.